KU-535-303

GENERATION GAMES

By the same author

A Parents' Survival Guide
A Marriage Survival Guide
Getting it Right: A Survival Guide
to Modern Manners

Fiction
The Man for the Job

GENERATION GAMES

LAURIE GRAHAM

Cartoons by Michael Heath

Chatto & Windus
LONDON

Published in 1990 by
Chatto & Windus Ltd
20 Vauxhall Bridge Road
London SW1V 2SA

All rights reserved. No part of this publication may
be reproduced, stored in a retrieval system, or transmitted
in any form, or by any means, electronic, mechanical,
photocopying, recording or otherwise, without the prior
permission of the publisher.

A CIP catalogue record for this book is available from
the British Library

ISBN 0 7011 3708 8

Copyright © Laurie Graham 1987, 1988, 1989, 1990

All these pieces, with the exception of the Introduction,
originally appeared in *The Daily Telegraph*

Laurie Graham has asserted her right to be regarded
as the author of this work

Phototypeset by Input Typesetting Ltd, London
Printed in Great Britain by
Mackays of Chatham Plc
Chatham, Kent

CONTENTS

Introduction vii

1987

from **Nights Errant** 1
to **Going Crackers** 44

1988
from **Teed Off** 46
to **Cold Comfort** 97

1989

from **Fighting Talk** 100
to **Festive Shades of Black** 160

1990

from **The Cinderella Shift** 162
to **Yesterday's Children** 189

INTRODUCTION

At the beginning of 1987, with my second book selling better than I had ever dared hope, I left my superannuated, interior-sprung, satin-lined job and became a full-time writer. Which is how I came to be poking the fluff from between the typewriter keys when my telephone rang and Trevor Grove of the *Daily Telegraph* said 'I've got an idea.'

'Generation Games' was actually conceived in El Vino's after two gin and tonics. The *Telegraph* thought people would enjoy reading about the life and times of an ordinary family. I thought they probably wouldn't. We agreed to give it a try. And the rest is now slowly yellowing history.

My son and three daughters generously supplied all the material. They never failed me. And my readers were quick to respond with cries of recognition. The world, it seems, is full of children who won't eat carrots.

This collection spans three years of great change. When 'Generation Games' started my children were pinkly innocent. We had a Ludo board, and a one-legged Action Man, and we never missed an episode of *Scooby Doo*. Now I have three adolescents, and one on the brink. Action Man has gone to find his leg. The Ludo has been put away for the grandchildren. And sometimes I don't sleep so well at night.

And have they minded this weekly public laundering of the dirty linen? They say not. It cheers me no end to discover that though they have forgotten everything I ever taught them about prudence and punctuality, they still have their sense of humour. With thanks for that and more, this book is dedicated to the Daughters, Senior, Middle and Junior, and to the Heir Apparent.

They tell me anyway that they anticipate that revenge, when it comes, will be ambrosially sweet.

LAURIE GRAHAM
April 1990

April 1987

NIGHTS ERRANT

I've been seeing this man. No, I've been *trying* to see this man. Every time we dim the lights, open a bottle and drag out the old Art Garfunkels we get gatecrashed by insomniacs with acne.

Being available to your children, to answer their questions and listen to their point of view is something we've always believed in. If you don't, we thought, you suddenly find you've turned into the kind of family that doesn't know where its kids are at night. Or who they're with. We know where ours are. Right here with us.

When we want to watch something of a sensitive and disturbing nature, likely to cause offence to some viewers, there they are, needing urgent counselling on blackheads or Ohm's Law.

They won't go away. I've tried lying horizontal in my pyjamas and yelling, but I think over the years we've simply been too friendly. If we were going to be the type of parents you don't wake up to talk about the threat of nuclear annihilation or what's going to happen next in *EastEnders* we should have started long ago. And we should have had their biorhythms seen to.

As soon as the weather man has done his stuff, they're wide awake and full of pertinent conversation. We call it the Kiss of McCaskill. World peace; eye-liner; Graham Dilley's bowling; and

whether toasted cheese sandwiches give you indiges-
tion if eaten late at night. You name it, we cover it.

Sometimes I feel quite disadvantaged, unless it's
eye-liner or Graham Dilley, in which case my
maturity and wisdom give me the edge. I just wish
they'd understand that I do have other things to fit
into my schedule. Like explicit sex. And toasted
cheese sandwiches. The kind of things best left until
after McCaskill.

RAT'S TALE

Don't talk to me about animals. I'm the kind of woman that doesn't even love the Andrex puppy. Our own stock has now dwindled to one rabbit that'd break your wrist as soon as look at you, so a certain amount of lobbying goes on. Photographs of Siamese kittens stuck on the fridge and that sort of thing.

But I'm not biting. Not unless I absolutely have to and if I absolutely have to I shall only be prepared to consider a pig or a rat.

Pigs are smart. I used to know a pig called Doris and she had zillions more brain cells than our Irish Setter. Not that that tells you much. Let me put it another way: she had more brain cells than all the Irish Setters in the world put together. So did her friend Elsie, and as pigs go *she* was pretty thick.

Rats are even smarter. Me and rats go back a long way. When I was a scientist some of my best friends were rats. I used to watch their oestrus cycles like a harpy, and when the moment came I bunged 'em in the bridal suite for a night with King Dick.

King Dick was straight off Mean Street. And yet some of those rats could spend all night with him and not get pregnant, which is what I call smart. After that I was ratless for years. There was a mouse that wandered in off the streets to eat our bedding. He wouldn't heed a friendly warning, so in the end I had to set a trap and lie awake sobbing until I heard it go *gerdunk*. But a mouse is not the same thing at all.

Recently rats have come back into my life. The Middle Daughter changed schools. Her new teacher

made her write with a proper pen *and* he kept rats. My heart warmed to this man immediately, and the Middle Daughter, a living legend of sunshine, spleen and bile, warmed to the rat.

By half term she was permanently stained with Quink, but I can live with that because she has also become one of the most useful crutches known to mothers of burgeoning youth – a human rat.

She is willing to rat on anyone, but principally she rats on the Senior Daughter. She ratted about my disappearing Estée Lauder Brush-On Blusher. She ratted about my vital research copy of *New Musical Express* that got hacked for a picture of some ephemeral hunk. And, best of all, when the Senior Daughter went to a birthday and we were still thinking it'd be bunny jellies and chocolate fingers, she ratted about the snogging.

Take my advice. If there's snogging afoot, get a rat.

May 1987

UP THE POLE

I wasn't in the Brownies, so the discipline of not leaving home without a safety pin, a sticking plaster and a large bell tent was never instilled in me. Having a mother who could produce a screwdriver at short notice on a train to Istanbul didn't help either. I relaxed and grew up to be the kind of woman who knows she has a spare lightbulb and a birth certificate somewhere, if you can just give her a few days to find them. Rush me and I'll blow it.

I think that's what the school is up to. I think they're trying to make me look inadequate.

The Heir Apparent and the Middle Daughter are Maypole dancers this year. I know this because every time we sit down to eat they start needling each other about which foot you start on for The Spider's Web.

May Day minus four, and counting. It has been announced that white shirts will be worn. This was not a suggestion. It carried the force of an Act of Parliament that's had the Royal Assent. But we didn't have any white shirts the right size because the school colours are blue. Furthermore, the Heir Apparent was not prepared to dance in the market square in a big girl's blouse, and who can blame him?

White shirts were borrowed. But we weren't through yet. 'The other thing is,' said the Lad, 'because it's a Victorian reconstruction I'm supposed to wear corduroy trousers and long grey socks.' 'But it's summer,' I whimpered. 'All that stuff has been put away.' 'Well,' he said, 'we shall have to do something because I'm meant to look like I'm wearing knickerbockers.' So I leaned into a deep, dark cupboard and fell base over apex whistling for woolly socks.

May Day minus one. Hair ribbons will match the dancer's skirt. I said 'Pardon?' and the Middle Daughter said 'Green.' We'd got a hideous purple thing on a hairslide, but we needed green. There was no sense in pretending. I was plumb out of green hair ribbon. Racked with anxiety, I lost a good five minutes' sleep over it.

May Day minus three hours. We secured the hair in a plain rubber band and hoped for the best. I said to the Lad, 'Thank goodness the colour of your shoelaces doesn't matter!' And he said 'I *knew* there was something I had to tell you . . .'

June 1987

A CAPTAIN'S INNINGS

First game of the season and I have to put my team's defeat down entirely to temperament. This is what happens when they've spent all winter watching Charlie Nicholas. I'm afraid I have no patience with it. It's hard enough making up the numbers.

We used to have neighbours who would join in. It may have been because we paced out the wicket right across their gateways and none of them could get their cars out and go anywhere, but I think they just liked whacking a cricket ball around. Nice crowd. Shame they all left. The new lot don't want to play.

So this year we've had to wait for the Aged Parents to visit before we had enough for a game of four-a-side in the back garden. I did the selecting. Whoever gets the Junior Daughter, an engaging child of limited attention span, has to be compensated with players of quality, so I let the Old Feller have Grandad and the Senior Daughter, mean fielders in the slips, both of them. This left me the Heir Apparent and the Also-Rans.

We won the toss and I put my mother-in-law on for her first spell. She got knocked all over the place. I brought the Lad on and sent mother-in-law to see if the washing was dry.

Grandad was really getting into it. We kept reminding him it was our garden and not Heading-ley, but still he kept skying them. We spent hours knocking on doors saying 'Can we have our ball back?' and Grandad would be at the crease still if I hadn't resorted to psychology. Just before he played a stroke I shouted, 'Anyone for a cup of tea?' He faltered, cracked it over long leg, and mother-in-law took it with one hand. All out for 321. Or was it 123?

I told the Heir Apparent to get padded up smartish because it was blowing a gale, but he couldn't. The Middle Daughter had run off with his equipment and was rolling round the outfield sobbing 'I *am* going to be Greg Chappell! I *am*!'

Bringing to motherhood the soft hand in the iron glove that was a hallmark of the Brearley captaincy, I said, 'Listen, you snivelling misfit, either be Geoff Boycott or go to your room.' She said could she be Dennis Lillee in the next innings instead, and as I was anxious for a result I said she could, but no bouncers, beamers, or bad language.

The Lad kept his head up and put on twenty-seven before he was dismissed by a lifting ball. I survived one foolish stroke, aided by the Junior Daughter who was busy at cover point, tucking her doll in its pram, and went straight on to play another, caught and bowled by the Senior Daughter. Mother-in-law was out for nine, teatowel fell on stumps. And Dennis Lillee was fourteen not out but sent for an early bath for answering back. I made next door's dog Man of the Match for the day's most lethal delivery.

AFTER A FASHION

From time to time my children like to get out the photograph album. Mainly they've been interested in themselves, and the odd shot of some dear departed dog or tricycle. Their interest in things that were going on before they were born has been slower to develop. But it has started. Gradually they are absorbing pieces of family mythology. 'Yes, those *are* platform boots your mother is wearing in her wedding photograph. And No, your father is *not* wearing a wig.'

The other day they turned up something really nasty. First, the hair. Heavy, henna-coloured curtains of it. Then the micro-kaftan, decorated with little bits of mirror. But worst of all, the trousers. Purple, snug around the thigh, and from the knee down, wider. Wider still and wider. An exponential leap in width. Result – invisible feet. The Senior Daughter nearly ruptured herself.

Okay, it's a fair cop. It was me and I was wearing flares. I was young, impressionable, everyone else was doing it, it seemed like a good idea at the time, and so forth. I'd like several other offences to be taken into account, including going equipped to offend in a Courtelle mini-skirt. I decided to sit them all down and make a clean breast of it.

It began with a beehive. I only wanted to see what it looked like. I came from a good home, never wanted for twinsets or nylons. But once I'd seen what The Ronettes could achieve with a comb and a can of shellac there was no stopping me. Dull, lifeless hair, split ends. It's a sadly familiar story.

Then the mini. It was never a particularly good idea because I was built like a stormtrooper, but those were wild, crazy times and there were worse sights around than me, just about. Significantly there are no surviving photographs of that phase of my life, but I've told the children anyway. Sooner or later they were sure to ask, 'What did *you* do in 1964, Mummy?'

Well, the world has a way of turning and minis have come back. Not that I'll be bothering this time. These days I'm built like a stormtrooper's mother. But I do like to see things come back. I said I'd never wear stilettos again, and I have. And pedal-pushers. My mother said I'd wear day-glo socks over her dead body but I wore them last year under her very nose.

The Senior Daughter said, 'Flares will never come back.' I think she's right. They are unrepeatable. Whoever designed them had been at the pop bottle, of that there can be no doubt. Everybody says *they* didn't wear them, but they did. Led Zeppelin were hard men and they wore them.

Some of us wrecked perfectly good trousers with triangular inserts so we could look stupid too. And those with spending power bought them mail order from *New Musical Express* for less than a fiver! Who'd have thought you could look such a ditz for so little money?

Regrets? I've had a few. One actually. I was too young for drapes the first time, and too old when they came back. I'd like to have done the whole bit. Bootlace tie, ram's head belt, electric pink Shawaddywaddy suit. Ridiculous. But as the Senior Daughter says, 'You wore flares. What's left to lose?'

INJURY TIME

Nearly time for summer. Up here we usually get it at the beginning of July and then again the first week in September – the week when everyone has gone back to school in extra-long gaberdine they're going to grow into.

The question is, what does one wear for a season that lasts three weeks? Luckily I don't move in the circles that have to worry whether a plastic mac is all right for Royal Ascot. The biggest crisis for my summer wardrobe is the Junior Daughter's Sports Day. Let me explain.

As a conscientious objector I really ought to stay away. With age you do start to see the point of certain things, like outsize dress shops and earplugs, but Sports Days are still lost on me.

I'm all for athleticism if it comes naturally. Indeed, I've learned that the swiftest way to get the Heir Apparent to perform any small domestic duty is to place it at the end of an Olympic-standard endurance test. As in 'Cycle to Aylesbury, swim ten lengths of the pool, three-leg it home with the partner of your choice and then strip your bed.' But I've never understood the three-line whip.

Why are sportsmen such sadists? Would they like it if the intellectuals organised an end of term Mastermind contest and *everyone* had to take part, even the ones who keep their brains in their Reeboks? They wouldn't. They'd bring a note from home. I feel an immediate bond with anyone who asks his mother to write and say he's not fit for hurdling. My mother would never do it. She still won't.

Apart from the rain, and the public address system no one can hear, the worst thing about Sports Day is the ritual jeering at people with asthma and fallen archs; the lame and the halt who show up for the Mothers' Race.

The Junior Daughter really wants me to join in. She still believes, with touching innocence, that I am God in a frock, invincible in thunderstorms, beauty contests and egg and spoon races. My only escape route is to go dressed as a casualty.

I hit on this quite by chance one year when I was disqualified at the start line for being inadequately corseted. A bit of lateral thinking and I was home free. The next year I wore a floral print cleverly accessorised with an eye patch and a walking stick. And this year, in recognition of the St John's Ambulance centenary, I shall be wearing a triangular elbow sling.

I know it's only a bit of fun. I know it's heresy not to be competitive, what with a leaner, fitter Britain and Margaret voted Head of House again. But sitting on damp grass watching the Hoop and Bean Bag Medley is as far as this parent wishes to push herself.

The Junior Daughter will probably prostrate herself in her little black plimmies and tell me that squillions of other fat ladies are going to do it. But nothing will make me climb into that sack and jump. Next year surgical stockings will be worn.

July 1987

HOME AND AWAY

I think there's something wrong with me. Whenever my children have to go away, sleep in strange beds, exist without the comforting smell of mother, they don't care. I never get messages in bottles, or have to drive through the night to succour a pining heart. All I get are phone calls saying, 'It's me. Can I stay another night?'

The Middle Daughter has just been on a school holiday, and it was when I went to see her off that I started thinking. All around me there were tight-lipped parents. And ninety tense children getting the 'Don't forget to send a postcard, wear a vest and eat up your greens' treatment.

They were about to set off on a week of adventure but you would never have guessed it. You could have cut the *Angst* with a knife, and I found out why. Most of those ten-year-olds had never been away from their families before. Their mothers were suddenly uncertain whether any of them could wipe their own noses, and their fathers were choking back the tears.

I could have understood if it was wartime. Buzz bombs and children with labels round their necks would make me sob too. But this lot were going to Cromer to draw fishing boats.

Daughter and I stood by her suitcase and I wondered what I should say to her. Take care? We love

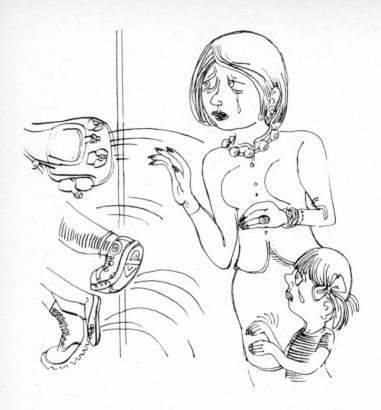

you? We seemed to have covered most of that during the previous ten years.

When it was time for them to board the coach there was much rending of garments and gnashing of teeth. There would be no little head on the pillow come bedtime. No roller skates on the stairs. Of course, she did leave a gap in the family. But life with a small, blonde version of Basil Fawlty can get you down and a change, as they say, is as good as a rest. It did cross my mind that dormitory life might not suit a girl whose bedroom I cannot contemplate without taking a very deep breath, but that was all. We got on with our lives.

When she came back she told us she'd been home-sick one night. For ten minutes. And her brother was man enough to tell her he'd missed her too. Then he went. Two hundred miles to a sports competition. Was he anxious, reluctant? He was not. Food parcels? Telephone calls? He said he'd try to find the time.

I thought, what kind of a joint am I running here? I don't beat them. I cook wonderful chips. How come they're always packing suitcases? 'Well,' explained my son, 'away seems more exciting. But,' he added, thieving my last piece of gum, 'coming home is best.'

Not a dry eye in the house.

COSTUME DRAMA

Raindrops on roses and whiskers on kittens you can keep. School uniforms are some of my favourite things. After years of explaining about glue and paint and tag-wrestling to three successive owners of a frilly white blouse, I've achieved a kind of liberation. All of my children now have to wear uniform. A different uniform for each child admittedly but every silver lining has a cloud. At least I shall never again have to get up early to discuss pastel velour with a child who is on hamster duty. Yippee!

We've all settled down to a simpler lifestyle. If the Senior Daughter has nothing to wear, I know I'm pretty safe ironing something black. For the Heir Apparent I beam in on royal blue. He would actually be happy to go to school in a dustbin liner. Well-dressed, to him, means carrying a Gunn & Moore bat, and grey polyester trousers are just another of those peculiar luxuries, like soap, that mothers waste money on. But dustbin liners are not approved schoolwear. It has to be blue and grey, and not to be confused with the Junior Daughter who is also blue and grey, but a different blue. These days I know my way round the blues and Royals better than a Whitehall pigeon.

Everything was under control. Until last week, when schools started to wish August would arrive, and the silly season was declared open.

First, the Middle Daughter, recently rewarded for learning how to sit on a horse and stay there, wanted to wear her new jodhpurs and boots to school for Showing Time. We never had Showing Time, did you? We didn't have an I Am Stuck Tray either. This is the face of education in the Eighties. I let her take them in a carrier bag.

Next, the Lad. A day in the Chilterns learning map-reading skills, for which he required a drink in a waxed carton and sensible clothing. It was a Wednesday. My day of the week for non-intervention. He dithered in his Y-fronts for a while and then chose a pair of jeans that have probably done him permanent internal injury.

Then the Senior Daughter, preparing for a week of extra-mural studies. 'All I need,' she said, 'is a pair of jazz-dance shoes, some new trainers, a silk scarf, and a long flowing skirt.' I said 'This is not Moss Bros. I am an artist, committed to writing a major comic *oeuvre* and I am fresh out of long, flowing skirts.' It was Thursday. My day for being the hysterical prima donna. 'Also,' she said, 'the price has gone up.' That girl has nerves of steel.

Finally, the Junior Daughter, who was going on a trip to a mansion. 'I have to wear Something Suitable,' she told me gravely. Ermine and pearls? Something sequinned? Or darned tweeds perhaps? We settled for a tracksuit that missed being smart by about two years. 'Wear this,' I told her. 'All right,' she said, a bit downcast. 'Is that because we don't have Something Suitable?'

August 1987

DISCOVERY BY DESIGN

This week I went walkabout in the City of London. I did it in the name of education, enlightenment, and the Senior Daughter's Religious Studies Summer Project: the churches of Christopher Wren. We started at Bank. It seemed as good a place as any.

St Lawrence Jewry is seen at its best approached from the west in full sunlight. We came upon it from the east and in rain. I thought I'd combine lessons in architecture with lessons in perversity. On then to St Mary-le-Bow. The Senior Daughter was already getting the hang of Wren, so I crept into the crypt to rest and be thankful.

The trouble with me is I'm easily diverted. The Monument was not on our list, but we climbed it – 311 steps of it – to the top. That's a long way to climb to confirm what you've always suspected about the City skyline in the 1980s. Christopher, old man, you're well out of it.

While we were up there I spotted another church, right under our noses: St Magnus the Martyr. It wasn't on our list either. But then I thought, 'Hold on! Serendipity is more my style!' And who can say what roll of the cosmic dice took us there and then to St James Garlickhythe where we fell into the arms of a lady who really knew her Wren churches?

And so, climactically, to St Paul's. Us and half of Scandinavia, Japan and the US of A. The first thing the daughter said was 'Cor!' and I had to agree. The grandiloquent scale of it. The ringing of the cash registers. Believe me when I tell you, we did St Paul's. Whispering Gallery, Stone Gallery, Golden Thingummy. And me with blood pressure.

The daughter took a whole reel of film and quite a lot of it related to Wren. I said 'What are you taking now?' because the camera was pointing at a safety rail. 'Post Office Tower,' she said.

We looked west to St Bride's and I made a decision. I was prepared to admire genius on the back of a £50 note, but what I truly needed was a pot of tea. I said, 'Learning is a haphazard business. Come with me to Soho and complete your education.' So we rode all the way to the fleshpots, averting our eyes from Live Sex Tonite and the expense-account bibbers trying to remember the way out of Frith Street and back to the office, until we found St Anne's, right there in the casbah.

The daughter said, 'Wren wouldn't be very happy with the way this has gone.' I said, 'Maybe. But look at it this way. We're only two minutes walk from the best patisserie in town.'

Serendipity, Sir Christopher. Am I right, or am I right?

SETTLING ACCOUNTS

I have a pay dispute on my hands. The Senior Daughter put in for a cost-of-living increase, and the rest of them followed her like lemmings. Her argument ran something like this – we were well past the date for annual review, August had arrived so she ought to start her Christmas shopping, and anyway, how could anyone expect a thirteen-year-old to live on a pound a week?

I've laid myself wide open to this. Bookkeeping is something I do on the back of old envelopes. I'm the kind of weak, vacillating creature that docks pocket money for bad behaviour and then buys everyone a Cornetto because it's wet, it's Sunday, and there's nothing to watch but *The Antiques Road Show*.

My first difficulty with pocket money is finding the right level. Some children seem to have an awful lot. Then I can't decide what it's supposed to cover. I know £1 a week at thirteen does sound a bit mean, but that's not the full story. We do buy absolutely everything she needs for school, and quite a lot that she doesn't. Like Walkman batteries. And *Blue Jeans* magazine. Actually, *I* buy *Blue Jeans*. I'm researching an important piece of journalism: The Teenager – Arbiter of Taste or Hormonal Cock Up? But I let her read it afterwards.

She opened the bidding at £2. For this she promised to keep herself in Clearasil and Madonna posters, save regularly, and never again steal my last postage stamp.

The Heir Apparent joined us at the negotiating

table with a blue plastic dog. Some people bank with a black horse. My son banks with a blue dog. It contained 47p and an IOU I'd signed and forgotten. This did not pass unnoticed by the Junior Daughter who arrived with a flock-sprayed rabbit full of small brown coins and what she thought was a very deserving case. Four children, and only one of them not hustling for an increase.

The Middle Daughter spends all hers on hair slides and when it's gone she lives on her memories. Takes after me.

We settled at £1.50 for the Senior Daughter, 30p less for the Lad, and so on, down the scale. *Plus*, fringe benefits of three meals a day, shoes, clothing and laundry, felt-tip pens, nail-varnish remover, newspapers that report first-class batting averages, prawn cocktail flavoured crisps, and permission to breathe.

But the Senior Daughter was still at the table looking like business. She says I've eroded her differential.

CAPABILITY NOTHING

I've got a book on gardening that I fetch out every year about this time. It always starts the same way. Someone invites us round for a gargle, we sit out in the sun admiring the sumptuous trusses of their *Lonicera serotina* and I come home in a perfectly foul mood.

According to my book what I should do is site my

cold frame and compost bin, set aside ten rods of well-mulched earth for vegetables, and use what's left to create a place of twisting paths, limpid pools and leafy bowers that is architecturally at one with the house. Why I keep falling for this I do not know.

For a start, we don't grow food. So far as my children are concerned anything that doesn't come in a plastic bag from Sainsbury's is highly suspect. Gardens are for water-pistol fights and quarrelsome games. No space for radishes.

The Junior Daughter and I did have a go with loofahs and pumpkins this spring. We got them to the planting-out stage and then a pigeon with a big mouth put the word about. 'Everyone down to Laurie's place! She's got loofahs!' So I've no heart left for lettuces.

Other things we don't have in our garden are bearded gnomes, Elizabethan rose arbours, the fountains of Versailles, Etruscan urns, or an orangery. What we do have is a very tired lawn, a dank corner that is the final resting place of various four-legged friends, and a flowerbed, full of lost balls and flowers that turned out the wrong colour.

The lawn has to stay. I did suggest gravel, but as they rightly point out, you can't play football or Hickstead Horse Trials on gravel. And I don't suppose it's very comfortable for rolling on, potato peeler in hand, yelling 'I'm not cut out for motherhood!' We keep the lawn. The bunnies' graveyard is another matter. We should do something with it.

The Old Feller would like a pond stocked with Japanese koi, and so would next door's cat. But we've also had a request for a basketball net, and what the two smallest daughters would like is a magic fairy dell, where they could eat unauthorised jam butties and watch out for Cobweb and Pease-blossom.

My book says a *Skimmia japonica* would do very well there. But an enchanted grove with a basketball net would make me very popular.

Then there's the horrible herbaceous border. I think what I need is a gardener. My friend Rae has got one. He sort of came with the garden.

Albert suffers from the kind of deafness that goes and comes at tricky moments – like each time she asks him to hang up his rake and retire. But he is brilliant at getting kites out of trees, he doesn't mind his canes being borrowed by decathletes, and you should see his begonias.

I could do with an Albert. That, and a green and secret place where the gin stays cool, the ideas flow, and cries of 'Help! There's no toilet paper!' cannot be heard. Or, we could get a flat with a window box.

September 1987

CROSSED WIRES

Can anyone tell me where it is written that the moment my telephone rings someone will need me to be Mother? It's a very strange thing.

I'm not talking about sticky, incontinent small fry.

My children are big people. Sometimes they're too busy for me. If the postman knocks with a Please Do Not Bend and I'm still in bed, no one wants to know. But one peep out of the telephone and I'm closely attended on all sides.

Mostly I use a telephone located at the hub of the house. I'm accustomed to background noise; the general through-traffic of children and bike wheels and stray dogs does not disturb me. My problem is the urgent whisper. 'Can I go to Trevor's to play pool and if his Mum says can I stay to tea, can I and what time do I have to be home?'

I can't cope with this while I'm doing business. And yet I'm quite a versatile woman. I can iron a shirt, dye my hair and watch *Cheers* all at the same time. I used to write a reply, like *Be quiet and wait*. That used to work. But now I get a note back that says *How long?*

I've tried explaining. I've said, 'You know Stephen's Mum works on the Safeway checkout? Well this is where I work. Don't interrupt.' I've tried being inaccessible. We haven't gone cordless so I can't lock myself in the john for important calls, but there is a bedroom telephone. I've shut the door, put up my *Woman at Work* sign, and guess what? Instead of hissing 'My zipper's jammed and can I have another breakfast?' they yell it from the bottom of the stairs.

For themselves, they are full of telephonic savvy. They know about Discline, not to mention Album-line, Storyline and Sportsline, and they certainly didn't learn about them from me.

They also know it's a great comfort to be able to

phone a friend and say, 'You know Major Industrial
and Household Uses for Iron and Steel? How many
have you got?' and, that if you dial 010507 you can
get the Republic of Panama without the help of an
operator. I suppose I should be thankful we don't
know anyone who lives out there.

I have a dream. My children will answer the telephone politely and efficiently. They will write messages on the message pad, not in the margin of the
Radio Times. When I take a call they will dissolve
away into respectful silence, and they will never,
ever, dial Russell Grant's number to check on the
planets or go to Australia, get homesick and call me
collect.

Then, some day, I shall have a secretary. He'll be
young, a whizz on the word processor, with a look
of Mel Gibson and the wit of Horace Rumpole. And
when I say, 'Harry, I'm talking to the Coast. Go
away and make me a hot fudge sundae,' he'll do it.

HOUSE CALLS

We're moving house. The Old Feller's got 300,000
miles on his clock, most of them edged with orange
cones, so we figure the time has come to move a
little closer to the grindstone.

I don't mind. To me, home is where the biscuit
tin is, and there are worse places than East Anglia.
I like plenty of sky. Newmarket seemed like a good
idea. Twenty-nine racing days a year, right on the

doorstep. We viewed a house big enough for us *and* guests.

The vendor's teenage son showed us round. He said 'I'm not very good at this,' and he wasn't. The children agreed that if we bought it they all wanted to sleep in the attic. This may have been because it was the only room not papered with Welcome to My Nightmare vinyl. But more likely it was because the access door was too small for anyone bigger than thirty-three inches round the hips. I thought of all those beds going spare. I was seduced by the idea of lodgers who knew their horseflesh.

And then there was the cellar. It was locked. No key could be found. In desperation a kitchen drawer full of tangled string and broken pencils was up ended and the Junior Daughter said to him, 'We've got a drawer like that at our house.'

He never did find that key. On our way out a small boy hung over the banister and said, 'Me Dad locked the cellar on purpose because I'm not to be trusted and I might go down there and drown in the flood water.' If he's still alive, I'd like to take this opportunity to thank him.

We drove to Cambridge, where compact means small and small means very small. And whichever way you cut it, a gasworks view is a gasworks view.

In the middle of a hot afternoon we found a gem. The house we'd dreamed of. Having found it we knew at once that it was too small. Several of us haven't finished growing. It was a shame, because the children loved it too, though I did have difficulty persuading them that the grizzled old labrador didn't come with the fixtures and fittings.

We finished the way we had started: with a locked door. This time we were asked to use our imaginations about a whole house. The key had gone missing, so what? This superbly restored brick and slate residence offered light and airy accommodation on three floors, according to the man without the key.

We shall never know the truth. Nice blackberries in the garden, if you enjoy fruit that grows at dog-leg height.

The search continues.

October 1987

A PLACE FOR EVERYTHING

The first two weeks of term, when everyone has
squeaky-clean gym shorts and lots of good inten-
tions, I get bitten by the same bug. 'I'll turn over
a new leaf,' I think. Change the sheets. Give the
bedrooms what Hilda Ogden would call A Good
Bottoming.

They say things are never as bad as you fear they'll
be. Why do they say that? The next time someone
says that to me I'm going to show them the inside
of my airing cupboard.

I tackled the Lad's room first. Before I had children I always imagined a boy's room would have a
model yacht on the window sill. I thought small boys
always had a model boat, a baseball glove, and a big
kite. My son doesn't. He does have something on
his sill and I will tell you what it is, but not before
I've told you that under his bed he had five pairs of
outgrown football boots, a cello string, a roll of
wallpaper, every book ever written by Willard Price,
and a very nasty smell indeed.

His is a small room. I lay on my stomach and
trawled under the bed with a wire coat-hanger. A
signed photograph of Oxford United; an Odor
Eater; and an apple core. Which at least explained
the smell. I was then faced with the problem of not
disturbing the residents. The Heir Apparent, a boy
at heart, but soon to be a man, has close on twenty
furry toys. He keeps them in an old sleeping bag and

the word *cull* is not in his vocabulary. He believes anything losing its stuffing is worth loving, and I'm not going to argue with him because that augurs very well for my old age.

I did argue with him about his sock drawer. A lump of Mount Etna, two cricket balls, quite a lot of corks and hardly any socks. The socks were in the trouser drawer, the trousers were in the shirt drawer, and the rest you know.

And there was still the window sill. It's little wonder I can never keep a window cleaner. There was the usual junk. Lengths of string. Joke scabs. But the conversation piece, I hardly know how to tell you, is plastic, lifelike, and last Christmas, when the Junior Daughter was getting sceptical about Santa Claus, it was used as evidence that a reindeer had passed our way and paused for a call of nature.

I said to him, 'In the interests of an Ideal Home, couldn't this live in the sock drawer?'

SPACED OUT

We've had science homework this week, the Senior Daughter and I. Seems like only yesterday we were doing dot-to-dot pictures of Paddington Bear. To be honest, I struggled a bit when she first asked for help, and I'm no slouch at Physics and Chemistry. This mother of four, Fleet Street columnist, and provider of boil-in-the-bag dinners is also a Bachelor of Science. With Honours.

Never mind how many years ago. A scientifically-

trained mind is a thing of precision and a joy forever.
I still know how to put a plug on a kettle.

But the Senior Daughter needed space exploration
– the human interest angle. Who went up there,
when they went, and what they did when they got
there. So I told her everything I know. And now
I'm going to tell you.

On March 16th 1926, Robert H. Goddard
launched the first liquid-fuelled rocket from Auburn,
Massachusetts. It travelled 184 feet in 2.5 seconds
and then went splat. This didn't tell us a lot about
life on Mars and Mrs Goddard would have been
happier if he'd taken up canasta, but it was a start.

In 1955 someone went seriously missing from
Journey Into Space. Was it Doc? Or was it Lemmy?
I can't remember. I got sent to bed. Then, in 1957,
the Russians launched Sputnik 1. We all stood out
in our back garden because my Uncle Raymond said
it would be passing by shortly, but we must have
been looking in the wrong direction. I missed Hal-
ley's Comet much the same way.

In 1961 Yuri Gagarin went into orbit. Once round
the block in Vostok 1. Remember Yuri? And Valen-
tina Tereshkova? I wonder what she's doing now?
Dropping stiff socks in the laundry skip like the rest
of us, I expect.

First man on the moon? Neil Armstrong. Space
person with the silliest name? Dead heat between
Gus Grissom and Buzz Aldrin. It's all flooding back
to me now. Shortest skirt beyond the edge of dark-
ness? Lieutenant Uhuru. Intergalactic proof that two
heads are not better than one? Zaphod Beeblebrox.

Once you've prodded the human brain there's no telling what it'll turn up.

I don't know that I'm properly appreciated. It isn't every mother who knows her Vogans from her Terrahawks. Next week, the Third Law of Thermodynamics. No problem.

HARVEST HOME

All is safely gathered in. I'm not in full possession of the facts, but at Harvest Festival this week I got the impression that we shall not be going short of marrows. I *had* heard that marrows are no longer the thing at Harvest Festival. I had heard that non-perishables are preferred, and I'd been glad, because I'd sooner offer thanks with a tin of spaghetti any day. And so, I guessed, would a lot of Senior Citizens. Time was when they daren't answer the door in October in case someone tried to give them another marrow.

We gave 'We Plough the Fields and Scatter' its annual airing, and some of the children sang it with feeling. Not ours, alas. They have only the vaguest idea of how bread gets to be bread.

I have tried to interest them in rural sights and smells, tried to get them to see the connections. Only this summer I said, 'Look! A combine harvester!' and then realised I didn't have any children with me. Just a carriage full of commodity brokers doing the *Telegraph* crossword.

Although we live in the country, we're frightened

to set foot in it. You only have to look at a five-bar gate and someone comes barrelling up in his four-wheel drive and screams, 'Rape! Don't you go trampling my rape!' Now when I was a girl . . .

I think my next book should be called *The Childhood Diary of a New Elizabethan Shire Girl*. We might need to tidy the title up a bit, but I have so much material, learned at my grandfather's side. We'd be up at first light to pick mushrooms for breakfast. My grandmother played safe with Weetabix because she didn't fancy a slow, painful death by toadstool. She was also wary of pigeons with their feathers on and milk that was warm from the udder. She had seen the future and she knew it was a supermarket.

When the Junior Daughter said we were invited to school and that after the hymns we could stay and buy back what we'd sent at an auction, I wondered what I should send. I said, 'How about a tin of meatballs, a packet of jelly, and another tin of meatballs?' She said, 'Can't you make some red jam, or a big loaf like a sheaf of corn?' She's our resident optimist.

I said, 'I can do you five rosy apples and a tin of meatballs and that's my final offer,' and she said, 'I wonder why only some ladies know how to make jam?'

I threw in a last-minute cabbage and held my head high.

SCHOOL REPORT

We've been back to school this week. Having found the house we want and checked on important points like is there a fish and chip shop close enough to get the battered cod home hot, and will Oddbins deliver, the next thing to settle is what we're going to do with the children.

My trouble is I always think I want what I've most recently seen. I must be an advertiser's dream. One forty-minute documentary on public schools and I seriously begin to believe that I want to spend £4000 a year so my son gets plenty of cold showers. All pie in the sky anyway. We have well and truly opted for the state system.

We started looking. We went to meet a head-master who wears lumberjack shirts. He seemed to know the name and life history of every child we met as we walked around his school. Mrs Thingummyjig, with a class of nine-year-olds, was letting rip at a little drongo who'd spent the morning picking his nose.

I love teachers who yell. I can really relate to them. The lumberjack said, 'The ethos of this school is the attainment of full potential by each individual, by whatever means.' I said, 'I know. I can hear it.'

Then there was the rest of the family to consider. Some of them not a million light years away from GCSEs and critical career decisions.

We went to look at a school that came so highly

recommended there was a queue forming outside with tents and primus stoves. I realised very quickly that the school was actually looking at us.

No lumberjack shirts here. The Head of Lower School looked like a regimental sergeant major in a Burton's suit. On our walkabout I had the feeling I was taking part in a royal progress with Ivan the Terrible. There was something in the air. Creative tension, possibly? Or naked fear?

The question is, will they have us? If only the Old Feller hadn't insisted on wearing that corduroy suit. And I just know I had on too much lipstick.

Still, *audaces fortuna juvat*. At least it did when I was at school.

A HARDY ANNUAL

This time each year we get invaded. For two consecutive weekends we can't move for hot-dog wrappers because the Charter Fair is in town.

It's not what it used to be. Four hundred years ago when they all came trundling into town with their geese and their gingerbread, there would have been plenty of space. I don't suppose the locals could have mustered more than a couple of oxen and an ass between them. Nowadays you're lucky if you find room to park a Montego.

I hate fairs. I might have liked the original format. Men in smocks. Warty women selling frumenty. You have to give credit where it's due, Thomas Hardy made some brilliant movies.

Fair Week must once have been an exciting time. The perfect excuse for getting out of the hovel for a few hours and catching a glimpse of the wicked ways of the world. A sort of medieval Langan's Brasserie.

The Senior Daughter hates fairs too. Without my saying a word she has picked up the advice I had dinned into me, that no good ever came of young women hanging around coconut shies. I can remember one or two who went home with more than a goldfish in a bowl.

The kindest thing to do with children who do like fairs is to give them some money and tell them what time to be home. But tattooed men in leather vests worry me, so this year, as before, I've insisted on accompanying them, except on the roundabout with the little cars, from which I am disqualified by weight.

Thankfully they didn't want to go on anything that involved being strapped in and turned upside down at speed. The Old Feller said, 'Go and see Madame Rosa.' I didn't see the point. I don't need a crystal ball to know that 1988 will be yet another year when my children won't eat spinach and I won't win the Booker Prize. I went though. She said 'I see many children. And you have a weakness in the chest.'

I told them, 'Madame Rosa says I should go home before bronchitis sets in,' which wasn't strictly true, but still . . . Dodged the dodgems. Didn't I do well?

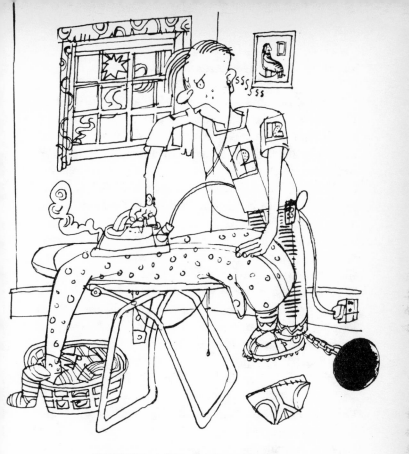

CRIME AND PUNISHMENT

There is someone in this family who has been in deep bother this week. I name no names. I hold to the Grub Street ethic that we are all entitled to our privacy so long as it doesn't spoil a good story. Suffice it to say that a bat, a ball and a pane of glass were involved.

Let me set the scene for you. It was an evening of wet leaves and wood smoke such as comes at the turning of a year. (I'm wasted here, you know. I should be writing travel brochures.) Anyway, it was a pleasant family scene. We sat listening to the death rattle of the central heating system, and the thud of a ball against an outside wall.

The cricket season had finished and there was someone out there at a loose end. Nothing to do but oil his bat and dream of whupping Kapil Dev for six. Straight through the window at the foot of our stairs.

When you have children you get plenty of practice at dealing with a crisis, and I knew I had to handle this one alone. Father was somewhere on the M25. Men always are when you need them.

The first thing I did was weep. I find this usually helps. Within ten minutes I was sufficiently recovered to start looking in Yellow Pages for Mr Fixit. Three of them didn't answer. Stuck on the M25, I suppose. But I did find a willing lad. He mended the window and charged me £20. He said, 'Best not to clean it until the putty has hardened.' I said, 'Will a year be too soon?'

Now the nameless person who had broken the window didn't have £20. Well he did, but it was inside Fort Knox. And I wanted redress. So the sentence of this court was that he should do a period of community service. An hour of ironing is worth £1. Emptying the dustbin is worth 10p. In this manner he is reducing his debt to society.

I asked my friend Ade if she thought I was being too lenient, and she said the word *draconian* sprang to mind. I wonder what she meant by that?

Meanwhile, a certain party has been drafting letters to the Howard League for Penal Reform. In between stints at the ironing board.

BLOWING IN THE WIND

I've got a heavy dose of those *When will it ever end, Can't get the washing dry, Blues*. The rotary clothes drier bit the mud. And why? Because lots of small people have spent the summer taking a ten-yard running jump at it and going Wheee! They said they were testing accepted theories of centrifugal force, but it looked to me like they were just going round and round until they felt sick.

At first it careened at a jaunty angle, and I pretended the inevitable was not inevitable. Then it keeled right over to port.

I wasn't actually in when it happened. I'd had to go to London to research deep-pan pizzas, so I had briefed the Heir Apparent as follows: 'When you get in from school, *before* you watch *Wacky Races*, check the washing on the line. If it's dry, bring it in.' I'm hoping that ten years of this will produce a man who does not think of women in terms of clean shirts.

When I arrived home the washing had not been brought in. He said, 'I think something kind of happened to the line.' And there it all was, lying in a sorry heap.

There then followed a vigorous exchange of views between me and the Old Feller. 'Why is it,' I asked, 'that in the era of the microchip tumbledrier we are still talking about lengths of rope?' He had an idea. He would re-set the old rotary line in concrete. 'I'll buy a galvanised bucket,' he said, 'and do it properly!' The last of the big spenders.

In the interim, a couple of days' worth of laundry

didn't get done. Eight shirts, twelve pairs of knickers, ten pairs of socks, and a few iffy towels. The
Lad didn't mind. In an emergency this is a boy who
can be relied upon to wear the same vest for a
fortnight. But the Senior Daughter has been con-
siderably inconvenienced. It's tough enough being a
teenager, without your Betty Boop sweatshirt going
out of circulation for an indefinite period.

I've decided to make a statement to the press. The
next joker I see hanging from my clothes line with
a smile on his face gets bread and water for a week.

Normal service will be resumed as soon as possible.

December 1987

A BIG FIDDLE

Have you read a book called *Which Instrument for Your Child?* You will, when you've lived with your mistakes as long as I have.

As parents we were unlikely to produce musical prodigies. We both have cloth ears and we weren't surprised when our firstborn struggled to get 'Jingle Bells' out of a xylophone. Imagine our feelings then, when we got a letter from school telling us that the Heir Apparent had symptoms of talent, and asking us what we were going to do about it.

He did have a plastic recorder, but we were soon put straight about that. *Serious* musicians learn orchestral instruments.

We had a quick shufty at the price tags in our local InstruMart and we got a nasty shock. Grandad kept saying, 'When I were a lad I could get a rattling good tune out of a comb and tissue paper,' but it was plain to see we were talking big bucks.

I was very reluctant to spend. My instincts told me that a boy who collects stamps, supports Luton Town, and reads James Bond stories till all hours was probably not going to show the kind of commitment that achieves conservatoire standard. We borrowed a cello. And he's been scraping away at 'Come Let Us Be Merry' ever since. Two years, or can it be three? Time flies when you have a song in your heart.

At first I thought I'd learn with him. I thought I'd

follow his lessons and iron out any little problems as they cropped up. But I never got beyond pizzicato. Demented plucking suited my temperament. Controlled use of the bow did not.

My role is now reduced to foaming at the mouth every time he ducks out of practice. His teacher says he's doing marvellously. I suppose she knows what she's talking about. All I ever seem to hear is the twanging of broken strings and cries of, 'It's your fault! I only go wrong when somebody listens to me!' Maestro Tortelier has clearly got competition.

And have you ever tried to take a cello on an Abandon Hope All Ye Who Pay and Enter bus? I said to the Middle Daughter, 'If it turns out you're musical you can learn to play the spoons.'

GOING CRACKERS

Father Christmas may be putting in his final appearance with us this year. The Junior Daughter seems very streetwise all of a sudden, and I sometimes wonder if the whole family hasn't just been humouring me for years.

I love Christmas Eve. You can keep those chestnuts roasting on an open fire, and little Aled Jones singing his socks off. You can even keep my Mum doing the washing up in a Groucho Marx nose, and the Boxing Day race card at Kempton Park. Christmas Eve is best.

Hanging up the colour-coded stockings. Burning a candle to signal to Santa that his double brandy is waiting for him. We left him a glass of port one year, but there was a note for us on Christmas morning. *Sorry. Daren't touch the stuff. Gout.*

And every year the same argument about bed-time. All the grown-ups needing to go to bed straight after supper, and all the little people wanting to stay up late and see the reindeer.

In our house Santa comes through the door. Even when we had a chimney I couldn't be bothered explaining how someone with a forty-inch waist could make it down our flue with a sack on his back. In fact, he's a difficult man to justify in many ways. Can anyone explain why all the shops start Christmas in August and he leaves everything till December 24th? Call me a female chauvinist, but I can't believe a woman would cut it so fine. And the Junior Daughter would like to know, will he be leaving her a marzipan pig again this year, because marzipan is not her best thing. I think she may be calling my bluff.

My friend Julia had similar problems last year. Helping her son to hang up his stripy stocking and make a wish, she said, 'Ssh! I think I heard sleigh bells. Did *you* hear sleigh bells?' 'Yes Mum,' he said, 'I think I did.' And then he zipped up his anorak and went out to get ratted with the rest of the ice hockey team.

TEED OFF

Until this week my most intimate association with the game of golf was knowing a cat named Woosnam.

Suddenly everything has changed. The Heir Apparent got golf clubs for Christmas. Proper irons, endorsed by the great Seve as being suitable for growing lads *and* – here comes my point – for middle-aged women. My attention was drawn to this while I was writing the cheque, but I was ready with an answer. I am left-handed. Those clubs were right-handed. So ended a close shave with golf – I thought.

Then a clever dick remembered something. I throw left-handed. I tiddlywink left-handed. But since I bat right-handed there was a good chance that if I could hit a golf ball at all, I would do it from the right.

I was taken into a field to find out. A crowd of youths gathered and, just as I addressed my first ball, one of them yelled, 'Tell yer old lady her shirt's hanging out!'

The clubs were perfect. I had to think of other reasons for not spending Sundays queueing to use a hole in the ground.

My excuse arrived, via a jumble sale, from Illinois, USA. It is called the 19th Hole Birdie Electric Putter: Wide Entrance Model for Beginners. It looks like a dustpan with a hole, and if you aim right, it returns the ball to you. You can do it on carpet.

You can do it at dead of night. Best of all, you can do it without standing in a public place and being disturbed by the rapier wit of some pustulous young rake.

Being able to play in my slippers has persuaded me a little. Do you think those check trousers come in size 40?

February 1988

HOME TRUTHS

When pressed, the Senior Daughter has been heard to say this in my praise: 'My Mum is all right. She's the same shoe size as me and she lets me borrow her earrings. She knows who the Pet Shop Boys are, and she can mend plugs so she's pretty handy. And she's brilliant at guessing what's going to happen next in TV programmes. Actually, that's quite an annoying thing about her.'

Tributes like that make me feel like a million dollars. And that's not all. I also have a son who believes I have celestial connections because I once shared a railway carriage with Steve Davis.

This week the Junior Daughter has been writing her family history. A hundred years is a very long way back for a young mind to stretch. All those people we never knew, living in places we've never visited, doing jobs no one does any more.

Of her immediate family she has had this to say! 'My Dad was born in Scotland. He has yellow hair and is quite old. My sister is an age of 13. She is very tidy. She was born in a hospital but I can't remember which one. My other sister was born at home. She is a snake.'

I should now explain that the Junior Daughter is heavily into Chinese astrology. In fact, as far as she's concerned, anything Oriental is good. Sometimes she won't even use cutlery.

'My brother,' she continues, 'is a rabbit. He is a

good runner but not as good as me. My Mum was born in 1947. I think she is a pig. She is an author. She types all day. Nearly all day. She has maroon hair and a brown eye.'

Which canny old scribbler was it who wrote: 'O wad some Pow'r the giftie gie us, to see oursels as ithers see us'? Burns! That's the name I was fumbling for. Born in Ayrshire. In the year of the haggis.

NIT PICKING

This will not make a light-hearted Saturday morning read, but we must all swallow nasty medicine sometimes. First, a little social history. When I was a girl, radios were called wirelesses, Preston North End were in the First Division, and only dirty children

got head lice. In fact, as I remember it – and I remember it well – there were three dependable indicators of a slovenly home life: impetigo, a leatherette flying helmet, and nits.

My father had a flying helmet, and, incidentally, he had bed bugs, but I never heard him mention nits. Possibly our family had already started to come up in the world. Certainly I never had them. My mother was always equipped with a bar of Derbac soap, and there wasn't a creepy-crawly alive that was brave enough to take her on.

Next, a few observations on the theory of evolution. My understanding of Darwin was that it took millions of years of sludge just to knock together a few trilobites, and that I was therefore unlikely to witness a whole episode of evolution in my own lifetime. But something is afoot.

In the space of thirty years head lice have stopped pestering dirty people and settled in cleaner pastures. I have a leaflet that says they cannot fly, jump or hop, so I suppose they just waited their chance and sidled across a Bailey bridge into Vosene Land. A major change of environment this. And not exactly what Darwin would have called cricket. Perhaps I should alert the Royal Zoological Society.

Finally, a cry of anguish. Why do my children only get head lice at inconvenient times? Like when they are going to stay with Granny, a kindly, helpful woman who believes leopards don't change their spots and that contrary, to modern rumour, head lice still prefer the unwashed. Is it really coincidence? Or do they work to some secret, vindictive plan? Delivery men do, so why not insects?

I think the answer may be to bring back the truly terrifying nit nurses of yesteryear. A little intimidation, a few pairs of rough red hands on the rampage, and the whole lousy population might get eggbound to the point of extinction.

I wonder if Darwin ever caught them?

March 1988

MACTHINGGY

I hear on the grapevine that Birnam Wood has been on the move again.

The Junior Daughter has just had her first encounter with the Bard. Isn't it wonderful that children get live theatre brought into school these days? I think Will Shakespeare would have thoroughly approved.

I did O Level *Merchant of Venice* myself. Well, I *think* I did. I do recall discussing whether Shylock was a pitiful victim of anti-semitism or a silly old ta-ta who was his own worst enemy. What I am absolutely certain of is that I've never seen a performance of it.

Aged eight, the Junior Daughter has started with *Macbeth*. Edited highlights. It took me a while to get the facts straight because she had remembered it in reverse order. 'The man,' she said, 'had a fight with another man and he put his head on a stick.'

I asked whether there had been a lady in it. She said there *had* been a lady, but her name was Tracey, not Lady Macbeth. Had there been any demented inspecting of hands by the light of a taper? No, she didn't think so. But a boy called Gareth had been sick and there had been witches. Now we were getting somewhere. 'Eye of newt and toe of frog, wool of bat and tongue of dog?' Yep! 'Adder's fork and blindworm's sting, lizard's leg and howlet's wing?' She wasn't too sure about that bit, and anyway, she asked, 'What's a howlet?' Walked into that one, didn't I?

The part she'd enjoyed most was when the trees moved. Me too. If anyone is thinking of offering me the female lead, forget it! I want to be that messenger. 'As I did stand my watch upon the hill, I look'd toward Birnam and anon, methought, the wood began to move.' Is that a spooky line, or what?

Her next intelligent question was, 'Did that story really happen?' Back to the encyclopaedia. Yes, it did. About 900 years ago. Also, 'Is his head still on a stick somewhere, and if it is can we go and see it at half term?'

I'm afraid I blame a lot of this on the violence in *Grange Hill*.

DRESSING DOWN

The Middle Daughter, who is ten – sorry, the Middle Daughter who is ten and *two thirds* – has decided to make an early start on the beastlier bits of adolescence. This is the only early start she has ever made in her life.

Overnight she has gone from nice cotton frocks by St Michael to improvisations on a theme by Zandra Rhodes and Rifat Ozbek. But I have to admit that she is resourceful. There are six of us in the house whose wardrobes she can raid, and she usually manages to create the look she wants.

Then she was invited to a party. The kind of party where you dance with boys. Wouldn't you say this is all a bit premature? Wouldn't you think ten-year-olds were still good for a couple of years of Pass the Parcel? As it turned out there wasn't a lot of fraternising. The boys just hung around the bowl of peanuts and the girls danced with each other, so perhaps things haven't changed so much after all.

But that is by the way. Our problem had come earlier. What should she wear?

She started with the Senior Daughter's hobbleskirt and a frilly blouse. She looked like a table lamp. Next she tried her brother's grey flannel trousers and one of the Old Feller's striped shirts. Sort of Annie Hall without the hat. Then came an hour of tears during which she wore her vest and knickers. Time pressed on, the sun was over the yard-arm, and decisions had to be made.

Someone graciously donated a pair of black ski pants, and the Senior Daughter had her lawyers draw up a lease-hire contract on a green and purple sweatshirt from Macy's, 6th Avenue. There was a swingeing Wear and Tear clause written in, but the Middle Daughter continued negotiations and closed a deal for the sweatshirt, a denim jacket, and a pair of suede shoes that had seen better days.

I walked her to the party with a sinking feeling. What if a butler answered the door and wouldn't let her in because of that jacket? But a butler didn't. It was a boy in peg-top trousers, and he told her she looked cool, bless his heart!

I was thinking. This is probably exactly how Zandra Rhodes got started.

AID FOR THE HEIR-SICK

The Heir Apparent has been laid up with flu, poor lad. I don't know which has been the greater source of suffering; the virus, or the standard of nursing in our house.

I must say in my own defence that I'm always willing to give practical help to the ailing. I'll run down to Boots for a bottle of Lucozade for anyone who asks me. It's the brow-mopping and grape-peeling I'm not cut out for. My bedside manner has earned me a place in the Ministering Angel Roll of Honour somewhere between Josef Stalin and Bette Davis.

First he went off his food, then he got very hot and stayed that way for five days and nights. I don't really believe in doctors. By which I mean to say, I think doctors should be left to do what they can for the mortally ill, instead of being pestered by people who are merely hot and not up to eating a chip butty.

As the days wore on and there was no sign of improvement I began to wonder whether I was being more neglectful than usual. If we had had a medical encyclopaedia I could have diagnosed something rare and pernicious, but we hadn't. A look in the medicine cabinet didn't help a lot either. Someone had left the top off the cold cure, and the only other things I could find were an empty sticking-plaster box and a bottle of Friar's Balsam. 'Why is it,' I wondered, 'that other families have shelves neatly stacked with triangular bandages and sterile gauze, and all I can ever find is a topless Night Nurse?'

On the sixth day things looked a little brighter. He moved from his bed to a couch and watched Lionel Blair doing charades on TV. Isn't it odd how we regress when we're sick?

On the seventh day he rested. Bored witless. I bought him a puzzle called Instant Insanity – a kind of dismantled Rubik's Cube that's supposed to take

weeks to solve. It lasted him all of half an hour.
Maybe I could get my money back. On the eighth
morning he rose early. He ate four bacon sandwiches, cracked a teacup, moved the line spacer on
my typewriter, and committed two acts of grievous
bodily harm on his sisters.

He is now as well as can be expected.

April 1988

THE SWEET TRUTH

I found a peppermint cream chocolate bar in my fridge, and I was just thinking, 'I wonder when I bought that?' when the Senior Daughter came and took it right from under my nose.

'This,' she said 'is my maths homework. At least, it's part of my maths homework. I shall need one of those peppermint-cream filled chocolate pyramids for the other bit.'

Did *you* ever study that kind of maths? I didn't. I can remember doing isosceles triangles, and I can remember writing FREDDIE AND THE DREAMERS on my logarithm tables. But I'm sure we were never allowed to get involved with chocolate.

The Senior Daughter explained it to me. She's doing Volume of Prisms and Pyramids. A prism is a solid form that has the same shape all along its length. Like a cream chocolate bar. A pyramid is a solid with any shape base, which comes to a point. It can contain peppermint cream, or the mortal remains of an ancient Egyptian, or anything really.

Her homework was to calculate the volumes of chocolate and see which was the best value for money. But first we had to get ourselves a pyramid. I went to Woolworth's. They have acres of chocolate bars in there. I got lost momentarily, and came out between the Easter Eggs and the Pick'n Mix. I found a girl and asked her if she had any pyramids, suitable for maths homework.

'Nah,' she said. It sounded very final. But she was a willing girl. What she lacked in solid geometry she made up for in salesmanship. 'We've got chocolate oranges,' she said. 'They're nice.'

I did find a pyramid in the end. We measured the area of its base, multiplied it by its height, and divided by three. I'm not sure why you have to do that last bit. The bar was easier. You multiply the base area by the height and then eat it.

Our investigation showed that the pyramid cost about twice as much per mouthful as the bar.

I could have told her that without a maths lesson.

WILD THING, I THINK I LOVE YOU

The Junior Daughter, nothing if not perverse, has waited until we moved to an inner city before taking an interest in nature. For nine years she has been knee-deep in wagtails and weasels and she couldn't have cared less. Suddenly, she's enthralled. Each little flower that opens, each little bird that sings, has to be looked at through a magnifying glass and given a name.

It began with a dead butterfly. A Small White. We told her it had breathed its last but she thought we were giving up too easily. She tried chatting to it. She tried putting it in a cardboard box lined with shredded toilet paper. And I daresay if she could have found a likely orifice she'd have tried mouth-to-mouth resuscitation.

Meanwhile, up in the *Clematis jackmanii,* some-one who had planned on having a dead butterfly for his tea was feeling thwarted. According to our birdbook, the blackbird is partial to insects. And when he's not happy, because someone has stolen his woman or his next meal, he emits a chattering yell which rises and then subsides with a few protest-ing clucks.

I can vouch for the accuracy of all that. In fact the Junior Daughter has alerted me to an interesting characteristic in the blackbird. When the sap is rising, he does a lot more yelling, clucking and aim-less pink-pink-ing than he does melodious whistling. Also, he does a terrific B52 impersonation.

Our book told us that his correct Latin handle is *Turdus merula,* so we had to take a break in our nature studies while the Heir Apparent explored every avenue of lavatorial mirth. Then, up in the creeper, a domestic tiff erupted. Our blackbird, still hungry and disappointed, was getting an earful of grief from Her Indoors.

'We're supposed to be building a nest.' 'But that girl pinched my tea!' 'You've had tea. You've had breakfast, elevenses, a heavy lunch and tea. Now build!' I've overheard similar conversations in the Hardboard Department of Texas Homecare.

The butterfly was taken to school for a second opinion, and the second opinion was that this was a butterfly beyond help. I suppose it's better hearing these things from a stranger.

There will be a brief Lying in State followed by

interment, and the blackbird will not be attending. He's grounded until the nursery is plastered.

THE UNKINDEST CUT

My son has grown up believing a haircut is something you endure in your dressing gown, on bath night, and that the first sign a haircut is about to happen is your mother standing at the top of the stairs, pudding basin in hand, screaming, 'Okay, who hid the scissors?' Until he was eleven he had never seen the inside of a barber's shop.

Then the Senior Daughter interceded on his behalf. She said my haircut made him look like a hippy. As if she'd know. I mean, *like wow man*, hippies were a thing of the past when she was still in her pram!

So he went to the barber's shop – my little lad with the beautiful golden hair – and he came back with bristles and bloodstained pieces of Kleenex on his neck. Not so much a haircut, more a massacre.

I know children have to grow up, but this was more than I could take. We reverted at once to the homespun look and I tried very hard to get the hang of layering. I can now see I should have bought myself some proper scissors before I started, but you don't always think of these things at the time. I gave him a haircut that looked like a moulting bison and I paid the ultimate price. My tools were confiscated and taken to a secret place of safety, and I was banned from the job for life.

I found a place where you can get a cheap cut because it's done by a student of hairdressing. I said, 'Can you trim this boy for me?' but the girl on the desk said, 'We don't do *trims*. We only do Creative Hairstyling.' I wished I hadn't asked.

Then I had another idea. He could try my hairdresser. They'd look after him. Wash his hair, cut it for him, blow it dry. And charge him £8 for the privilege. Eight pounds for one very small head! At first I didn't believe him. I made him turn out his pockets to prove he hadn't spent a fiver on marbles.

And that was only the beginning. One session in a unisex salon has opened his eyes to styling mousse, contouring gel, high-rinsability shampoo, deep-penetration conditioner, regular use of the comb, *and* the attractions of the opposite sex.

At least with a pudding-basin cut he could keep his mind on Arsenal, the Pet Shop Boys, and Einstein's Theory of Relativity. Why is progress always such a mixed blessing?

May 1988

FIRST FORM OUTING

By some appalling piece of mismanagement, the Junior and Middle Daughters' Easter holidays lingered on and impinged upon an important date in any woman's diary – the first race meeting of the year at Newmarket. I was faced with a choice. We could stay at home and play snakes and ladders, bake gingerbread men, wish something exciting would happen in our lives. Or not.

Granny called long-distance and made her position clear by donating a recipe for gingerbread, followed by a few well-chosen words on the evils of gambling. There was really no need. If my children have learned nothing else from me, they have learned not to kill spiders and never, under any circumstances, to back horses so early in the season.

Education by stealth was not my intention. All I hoped was that the rain would hold off and we'd enjoy ourselves, but the Middle Daughter showed more mental agility with the Odds Indicator Board than we have seen in six years of blood, sweat and Fletcher Maths. And the Junior Daughter became sharply observant. 'If you turn this,' she said, with her finger on a knurled knob, 'the binoculars go cloudy. Steve Cauthen doesn't sit on his horse the same way Willie Carson sits on his. And that horse needs to go to the toilet.' Correct on all points.

In the matter of horseflesh, both daughters opted for the Silly Name method of selection. They had

Winking Winner marked as a dead cert. At the end of my racegoing life I shall probably agree that this technique is as worthwhile as ruining your eyesight reading form books.

In certain matters though, my daughters will concede I know what I'm talking about. When I say you'll be cold without your scarf, you will. And when I say a nicely priced little maiden is going to win, he will. But only on the day I'm definitely not betting.

PRESENTS OF MIND

Lists for birthdays are all the rage in our house. Instead of waiting to be asked, instead of waiting to be told whether she's even going to be allowed a fourteenth birthday, the Senior Daughter started her list early in February and is still at it on a long roll of paper, with changes being made by the hour.

Each addition is helpfully annotated; *Whitney Houston's latest album – NB: only ten shopping days left! Navy socks – not school socks, just really cool socks.* She has even made provision for extended credit. *Remote control colour television – this can also be my next Christmas present and the next birthday after that. If it's going to cost more than that, forget it.* We did a deal on the television. We agreed to forget it.

Lists are very sensible, aren't they? I mean, if people keep ignoring the fact that you've outgrown Lego and now have a serious eyeshadow habit, a list really is the best thing. Then, even though your

Aunty Vi will continue to buy you Andy Pandy handkerchiefs well into your forties, you can depend on getting a few of the things your heart desires.

So what's the matter with me? Why do I feel sad? If people don't want wonderful surprises, what's it to me? I can give up secret shopping trips. And hurried wrapping sessions with a chair jammed under the door handle. I should be grateful they played along with it for a few years. They did humour me. Up to a point. 'The nozzle is missing off the hoover.' 'I think I saw it under the bed, between the cunningly disguised snooker cue and the roller skates wrapped in Flying Snowmen paper.'

Of course, without a list, anything can happen. Without a list someone might buy you something truly amazing. You might get a framed hologram of a werewolf, or a pair of Zulu earrings. You might even get a giant chocolate chip cookie with your name on it.

Reason tells me I should welcome lists. They have so caught on that the Junior Daughter has started hers already, with only eleven months to go to her next birthday. At this rate I could do several years' shopping in one afternoon. Think of the time I'd save! I could finish *War and Peace*. No I couldn't. It wouldn't save me that much time. And I'd still feel drawn to shops that sell inflatable gorillas. For the girl who has everything.

June 1988

FAREWELL TO BALLS-ACHE

When you have a fourteen-year-old in the house, decisions of magnitude have to be made. Are the next two years of her education going to take an early lurch in the direction of science or the humanities? Or should a balance be struck? Can a balance be struck? And is it really twenty-seven years since I was making these very decisions myself? Fourth Year Options are the nettles we must now grasp.

When I was fourteen I turned my back on languages and practicalities. I could have learned to cook semolina and stitch run and fell seams. I could have read Balzac and Anouilh. But I prepared myself for a life of writing, cooking and fitting new zips in designer denims by signing on for every science course going. With the Senior Daughter it's different. She's sensible. I have the experience. Together we make quite a team.

I said, 'What about British History, 1688–1815? Or Classical Studies? You could learn to analyse and evaluate, detect bias, present reasoned argument, and make valid comparisons by taking Classical Civilisations in Four Parts. It says here.'

She said, 'I think I'd do better developing data collecting skills, mapping, graphing, communicating with others and learning to think for myself, whilst engaged in a course based on issues.' Geography. You don't colour maps any more in Geography.

You tackle issues and go on field trips to London Docklands.

Then there is Craft Design and Technology, which sounds very dynamic and relevant. In my day it was for boys only, and there was a choice. There was Metalwork and there was Bunking Off From Metalwork. Today you can work with plastics and electronics, even if you're a girl. But the Senior Daughter is opting out. I said, 'Well at least do Art,' thinking it would provide a bit of light relief from acid rain, depleted ozone layers and a generally heavy geographical scene, but she wants to do Child Development – a course devoted to parents and children, roles and needs, for which neither help with the homework nor pertinent examples should be hard to find.

She doesn't want to broaden her horizons. Not yet anyway. She wants GCSE Home Economics and a job with children. At the moment. Whereas her friend Twig plans to become a revolutionary.

I said, 'What's Twig choosing?' 'Modern History, loads of languages, stuff like that,' she said. 'You'll be able to talk to her about all that Balls-ache and Ennui you're always wishing you'd read.'

I wonder which course teaches tact, diplomacy, and French pronunciation?

ON PARADE

As a parent I have my faults. Sometimes I run out of name tapes, or don't have to hand a book on sugar-beet farming. Sometimes my fuse is a bit short. And sometimes the cupboard is so bare we have to eat at the hot-dog stand. But there is a brighter side to this story. I never cry over mud, ink or spilled milk. And every Saturday I buy a catering-sized bottle of tomato sauce.

Nor do I subject my children to public indignities. Young Maureen Lipman was made to stand on a sideboard and sing, and as things have turned out we're all glad she was. My children have been let off scot-free.

The only time I persuaded them to enter a fancy-dress competition I got the time wrong, and we arrived just as the winner – Mary Mary, with seed packets stitched to the hem of her frock – was climbing into her Dad's limo to escape the North Buckinghamshire *paparazzi*. We had tears from our Drury Lane Flower Girl and our Bluebell Fairy. And the Heir Apparent, who had put on a swimming cap and a large cardboard box and been transformed, against his better judgement, into a turtle, didn't speak to me for the rest of the weekend. I suppose it was tough enough being a turtle without the added humiliation of arriving when everyone else has changed back into their tracksuits.

They have grown up without a single Bonnie Baby Contest or compulsory Frank Spencer impersonation in front of Auntie Connie. All I have asked of them is that they present themselves, without sniggering, for introduction to visitors who do not know them. They are not required to curtsey or shake hands. Provided they stand still long enough to be identified and refrain from nose-picking, I am contented. But they are not. They don't like being summoned and made to line up. They say I've watched *The Sound of Music* too often.

I said, 'Fair enough. I'm a reasonable woman. Introduce yourselves. Say, I'm the Middle Daughter, I'm nearly eleven, and if anyone fancies a game of Dingbats later on you'll find me downstairs.' But they didn't go for that idea either. What they had in mind was to make a brief appearance, silently refuel with peanuts, and disappear fast. So I've threatened them. Either they accept the simple civilities of life, smile and say Hello, or I choreograph the whole thing. Music, costumes, lights. We could make the Jackson Five look like amateur night at the scout hut. As long as they're not too heavy for the sideboard.

BIG EATS

I'd like to talk about Liberty Hall. This is what comes of having a large family and a soft heart. People drop in to be fed. 'The more the merrier,' they think. 'Tell Cook to roast another ox.' After all, if you've been such a schmuck over contraception, you'll never notice another nine for supper.

I must confess that on occasions I have lost the ability to count. In the days when I used to ring a bell to get my children in from the street and up to the table, a woman once came to the door and demanded the return of her daughter. I denied all knowledge of the child, until the Senior Daughter tugged urgently on my sleeve and whispered, 'She's the one who just ate three burgers and the skin off the rice pudding.' Sometimes I just lose the will to count. But usually I know exactly what I'm doing. What I'm doing is feeding six, not running an army field kitchen.

In the name of motherhood I've put out the Welcome Mat for tadpoles and orphaned hedgehogs, and even been kind to hairy dogs with learning difficulties. But coach parties are something else. Friends turn up, with their children and their pets and their distant relations from Tasmania. They say, 'We know you weren't expecting us, so we brought you this,' and stick a pint of milk in my hand.

According to the cookery writers what I need is an Emergency Store Cupboard. Clement Freud recommends being prepared with a tin of artichokes and a jar of stem ginger. Funny how a man who is so sound on onion soup and proportional representation can be so silly in other respects.

Forget the tinned artichokes! We are talking serious quantities here. If someone says 'Chicken', I think 'Emu'. We are talking supermarket trolleys, and lots of folding money.

Of course, hospitality does bring its rewards. I *do* like to hear people murmur, 'Such talent! Such charm! And such big saucepans!' But what I'd really love is to be invited back and know I can accept without anyone crying, cracking up or calling in caterers. We'd even bring our own spoons.

July 1988

ON THE MEANING OF BREAKFAST

'Did you know,' said the Lad, fiddling with his egg, 'I have been alive 4,645 days?' 'Gracious!' I said. 'Doesn't time fly? And what is *wrong* with your egg?'

He said there were wobbly bits in it. Twelve years old, capable of advanced arithmetic at seven in the morning, and he's whingeing about a wobbly bit in his egg. '4,645 days,' he continued, 'is 6,688,800 minutes. I've been alive more than six million minutes.'

I showed a motherly interest in his calculations and threw in a little biology for free. 'It isn't a wobbly bit,' I explained. 'That's where the chicken would have grown if the egg had been fertilised.'

That was a mistake. Apparently wobbly bits are bad enough when they're an unknown quantity. To associate them with the private lives of cocks and hens while people are eating is not done.

We have a friend who keeps hens. I used her to illustrate my little story. Her girls keep on laying even though the cockerel spends all his time patrolling the perimeter fence and auditioning for *Le Coq d'Or*. And there are never any chicks.

'If hens lay eggs anyway, why keep a cockerel?' asked the Junior Daughter, who likes whites but not yolks. 'To annoy the neighbours,' said the Middle Daughter, who likes whites, yolks and wobbly bits. 'And why aren't there ever any chicks?' asked the Lad. 'Because,' I said, 'those eggs have a neglectful mother, who goes to literary lunches as like as not, instead of sitting on them and keeping them warm. Why is your pocket calculator in the margarine?'

'You have been alive 14,755 days,' he pressed on. 'I'll just see how many minutes that is.'

I scraped his uneaten egg off the plate and was overtaken by a great melancholy concerning time and fate. In a manner of speaking we all start out as wobbly bits. Some of us become Einstein and live for more than 29,000 days. And some of us become breakfast.

As I said to the Regius Professor of Existential Philosophy only the other evening, 'It certainly makes you think.'

MOTHER SUPERIOR

I hear I can stop worrying about not being a goddess. Phew! Sirgay Sanger, an American child psychiatrist, has been beavering away for ten years on the effects of working mothers on the psychological development of their children. His conclusions are that the children of working women are *privileged*. Sirgay Sanger, where have you been all my life?

When I first became a mother, back in the spring of '74, John Bowlby was still waving a big stick at working girls.

For those of you too young to have known Bowlby I will paraphrase. 'Anything less than full-time parenting, one-to-one, will blight your child's development and add yet another anti-social, psychologically impoverished vandal to the seething hordes.' Also, someone has to stay home to let the plumber in.

I have to tell you, I fell for this. For ten years I stayed home. I made playdough. I did foot paintings. Sometimes the children even joined in. And the only work I ever did was work that could be done within earshot of the pram. Those poor children.

I can see now that they must have longed for me to go on a very long journey. They probably had little conferences after Lights Out. 'Why doesn't this woman leave us in peace with a nice babysitter?' 'Maybe if we saved up and bought her a briefcase she'd take the hint?'

Eventually, after the youngest went to school, I did stick my nose outside. By which time I didn't even know how to apply for an Underground season ticket, and who'd give a job to anyone like that? Anyway, I still wasn't convinced that John Bowlby wouldn't come and drag me out of the office to show me that my neglected children had started biting their nails.

I persevered. I wanted to be a good mother, but I didn't want to turn into the sort who gets lonely when they all have to stay late for rounders practice. The Senior Daughter took me to one side and told me, 'Don't worry. We're fine. Besides, we prefer frozen dinners. They're more . . . reliable.'

And that's how it's been for the past four years. Frozen dinners, and me having nightmares about John Bowlby. But Sirgay says it's all right. He says I can delegate, and still sleep at night.

Anyone want to buy a pedestal?

FAIR HANDS AND FOUL

As a left-hander I have had my share of trouble in handwriting classes. The Dark Ages had just about wound up when I came along, so nobody actually asked me to change hands, but that was as far as their charity extended. I tried very hard. I even did extra practice. Still my letters trudged down a 1-in-5 slope in a most unattractive manner.

'Straighten the paper, that girl! Hold the pen correctly, and don't slouch!' Thwack! An excellent method of teaching a child to hate pens, ink, poems by Lord Tennyson, and people who get prizes for calligraphy.

Finally I found my own solution. An inspired tradesman opened a shop in Beak Street that sold left-handed pens. Imagine!

When I had children, I waited to see their handedness the way other mothers wait to see the colour of their children's eyes. They all chose their right. Correct, dextrous, adroit, all four of them, in spite of having a sinister mother. One aspect of parenthood I needn't worry about, I thought. My walls will be plastered with Odes to Nightingales and Certificates of Merit for Joined Up Writing, I thought.

The Senior Daughter shattered these dreams by adopting a style too small for the human eye. The bigger she gets the smaller she writes. Diminutive, squidged-up words. I worry about the significance of it. Have I repressed her? Does she think no one wants to read what she writes? Have I deprived her of nice big pieces of paper?

The Middle Daughter won't be writing *her*

memoirs on the head of a pin. Her mission in life is to cover planet Earth with ink. Smudges, thumb prints, gargantuan inky words that undulate across the page. I shan't interfere. I believe I may be the only living writer whose mother turned up at a book-signing session to check her handwriting.

One paranoid scribbler is enough for any family.

August 1988

PIG IGNORANCE

Watching the Six O'Clock News with children is always risky. There is usually a story that I feel unwilling or unable to explain. I mean, what *is* the European Monetary System? And are the Prime Minister and the Chancellor of the Exchequer really best buddies, cross their hearts and hope to die in a cellar full of rats, or could it be that they are pretending?

Anyway, there we were the other evening, huddled round the flickering screen, Gran, three children and me. The Junior Daughter was upstairs with her box of paints. Sue Lawley took us gently through the balance of payments deficit, the rising stars of the Cabinet reshuffle, and the wettest July since 1939. 'Later in the programme,' she said, 'the pigs who are on their way to Japan.'

Now the Junior Daughter is very fond of pigs. She collects pictures of them, and refuses to eat sausages. So do I, but not because of their pig content, which seems to me to be negligible. Her reasons are sentimental. She will not eat an animal she believes to be clean, intelligent, and greatly underestimated.

She even makes little piggy models. We went to the modelling materials shop and asked for Pig Pink, but the foolish salesgirl offered us something the colour of Day-Glo socks. The world is full of people who don't understand about pigs. Still, it seemed that pigs were about to make national news. We summoned the Junior Daughter to leave her paint pots and come see.

At Usk, in South Wales, young offenders are learning the rudiments of pig farming with a rare breed, the Berkshire. We saw them caring for the piglets with encouraging tenderness. 'He's killing it!' cried the daughter. 'No, no,' we comforted her, 'he's giving it a vaccination so it will grow up strong and healthy. *Then* . . . '

The point of the story dawned on Gran just before it dawned on me. The Berkshires of Usk are going to Japan because Emperor Hirohito likes them so much. Mainly he likes them well-roasted and carved very thin.

All diversionary tactics failed, needless to say. We might have retrieved the situation if it hadn't been for all that footage of gravy being ladled over *Loin of Berkshire Japonnaise.*

Tears before bedtime. Again.

KEPT POSTED

I hate to rub salt in the wound during this season of sealed mail-boxes, but aren't letters a lovely way to start the day? My optician writes to tell me it's time we talked: Mrs Cattermole of South London writes, with good wishes and a picture of pigs for the Junior Daughter; and the Milk Marketing Board writes, to the man who lived here before we did.

Like every other householder I get a lot of unsolicited trash as well. On a normal morning it goes from the doormat to the dustbin in one beautifully choreographed movement. It's only on very bad days, when it's too wet to peg out the washing and I don't feel like being a lady writer, that I fritter away ten minutes in opening it and reading it.

The Senior Daughter gets quite a lot of mail, and deservedly. She answers letters promptly and she answers them well. Unlike her brother. The only letters he writes are Thank Yous and he doesn't do those unless restrained in ankle clamps and threatened with the withdrawal of all televised soccer. He did have a penfriend once, but the poor lad probably died of a broken heart. All that one-way traffic in Australian stamps and postcards of Queensland must have got him down in the end.

Imagine then my surprise when *I* received a letter from the Son and Heir. No envelope. Just a sheet of my best quality A4 weighted down with a mug of cold coffee. *Mum*, it ran, *while you were at the shops we had a bit of bother. They said I was messing up their game but I wasn't. The thing just came off in my hand and it must have been very loose anyway.* Appended to this was a footnote from counsel for the prosecution; *Oh no it wasn't loose. And he had two toasted tea cakes without asking.*

That was only the beginning. The leaving of notes has caught on in a big way. Apparently I've become such a tyrant no one dares speak to me any more.

Dear Mum, wrote the Middle Daughter, *I don't mean to be a nuisance or anything but they say they're going to grass me up if I don't tell you about my leotard. I promise to look everywhere for it. Also, they called me a word.*

No we didn't, said the postscript, proving yet again that letters are a lot safer inside sealed envelopes, *We called her two words*.

Junk mail with a difference, you might say.

UNDERWHELMED

We had our chimney swept last week, very early in the morning so that Walter's parked van wouldn't bring all of Cambridge to a standstill. Anyway, he likes to get up and get on. When Walter says seven thirty he means seven.

Two children slept through the whole event, and the Old Feller sleepwalked in search of a clean shirt, while Walter and I looked at the Four Day declarations for the St Leger. Then he made a start.

I said, 'Who wants to go and watch for the brush?' and a small girl with her elbow in the butter said 'Whatever for?' Of course, quite exciting and interesting things can sound extremely tedious when they're explained at length, and watching for a sweep's brush does rate fairly modestly on the scale of great experiences. Still, I was not prepared for such a jaded response. I went to watch for the brush myself.

'You be careful,' said Walter. 'Don't you run

straight across that road without looking.' And while I was over there, giving Walter a small ovation as his brush emerged, I wondered what I'd done to breed such sophistication in my children. It's not just sweeps' brushes. They don't care about riding on open-top buses any more either. They don't rush to the window when they hear a fire-engine coming.

I do. And they look at each other and think, 'What an odd thing to do.' Which brings me to another simple pleasure. Mexican Jumping Beans. I still like them. How come children don't?

Overlooking the well-known fact that at parties these days young guests expect a Golden Handshake in the form of at least a fiver's worth of trivia, I went to a shop and bought jumping beans. Our host child warned me that no one would see the point of them. She said digital watches or Rick Astley T-shirts were more the sort of thing, but I stuck to my guns because I believe it's the thought that counts. Besides, who has that kind of money?

'What do you do with these?' asked Demelza, the departing guest. 'Don't bite them! Don't stick them up your nose!' I screamed, 'Just put them in the palm of your hand and watch them.' Confirming to all present that the Middle Daughter is to be pitied for having a mother who is a stick short of a bundle.

Walter says he blames it all on central heating.

October 1988

CLOSET CRISIS

I am not an unreasonable woman. As a family we're going through a difficult time, what with the six of us and the itinerant band of carpenters, electricians, plasterers, deputy plasterers, deputy plasterers' assistants, and unidentified men with pencil stubs behind their ears, all sharing the small cupboard we call the bathroom.

I mean, everyone has to use the bathroom, right? Certain functions cannot be avoided. If your eyebrows need plucking, they need plucking, and there's no sense in fighting the inevitable.

On the other hand, if it's the lavatory you need and the surveyor is standing on it, there are always the bus station facilities a convenient three minutes' walk from the front door and handy for checking out the coach service to Ipswich at the same time.

With a little flexibility and foresight it should be perfectly possible to live with strangers and bathrooms that can be reached only by ladder. So do I get co-operation? Next silly question?

The two youngest members of the family have done their bit. They have both volunteered not to wash for the rest of the year. Similarly, the Heir Apparent has pared down his *toilette* to one shower a week or on receipt of complaints, whichever is the more frequent. And he doesn't need a mirror. A quick brush of the teeth and a glance at the sports page and he's set up for the day.

The mirror-hog, who monopolises the shelf space and refuses to come out for hours, is the Senior Daughter. On a good day all she has to do is cleanse, tone and nourish her complexion, wash and style her hair, and perform a thorough pedicure. But on a bad day . . .

'It's horrible!' she says, through the closed door, 'My skin's horrible!' How can you live with people like that? *My* skin's horrible. I've got a pension plan and a hairdresser who keeps asking if I'd like something to cover the grey, and still my skin thinks it's adolescent. Do *I* go around gnashing my teeth and locking desperate people out of the bathroom? Where has she learned this obsessive preening?

I've told her, 'It doesn't matter that you're growing a second nose. You have a lovely personality.' And I've said, '*Never* look at your skin in a magnifying mirror. No one was ever meant to see themselves that way.' But the girl is inconsolable. Also, she thinks someone has been fiddling with her Exfoliating Scrub. The plasterer, probably.

Now tell me, wouldn't you say forty was a bit young to be going grey?

THE GRAN TOUR

The Lad is off to foreign parts next week. For the last time before GCSEs we're letting him out of school to chaperone the Wandering Grandmother.

Gran has been a late developer. She was all of fifty before she started sending postcards from the

Hindu Kush. Now there's no stopping her. I only have to wonder out loud about some ravishing chocolates we once ate, and she's airing her suitcase. 'I'm sure I bought them in Copenhagen. I'll see if I can get some more, shall I?'

So she and the only begotten grandson are heading south, in search of sunshine and early Christian catacombs. Very nice too, you might think. Now for the problem.

Since April my son has been master of his own wardrobe. After a lot of begging and wild promises he now has a weekly allowance. Eight pounds a week to provide himself with *mufti* for every occasion. In his first flush of wealth he bought *The Martian Chronicles,* gifts for all his sisters, and some pretty fabulous fibre tip pens. I hate to interfere.

'Make a list of what you need on holiday,' I said. 'Then make another list of what you've got. Subtract one list from the other and do what's necessary.' 'Right,' he said. 'I've got eight pairs of grey woollen socks . . . ' I caught a glimpse of the man he's going to become. The kind of man who will honeymoon in Bali wearing grey woollen socks. ' . . . and eight T-shirts,' he continued.

Now I don't want to seem negative, but he doesn't really have eight T-shirts. He has eight floor cloths with sleeves. 'What about Evening Wear?' I asked him. 'What about something suitable for escorting a grandmother to dinner?' and I watched the colour drain out of his face.

He nipped out to the shops. I suppose he had to learn sooner or later that beachwear sells out in

May, and by September all you can buy is Christmas cards. Rags will be worn this autumn.

A HAPPY EVENT

I have recently become a grandmother. Luckily for all concerned it happened at such short notice there was no time for any knitting, and as it is to be a temporary state of affairs I've decided against anything flamboyant, like buying Premium Bonds or laying down port.

This episode in my life began when the Senior Daughter chose Childcare and Development as one of her GCSE options. I thought it was an excellent choice. High time someone in this family understood the theory behind all my gaffes, blunders and weekly fits of the screaming abdabs. In return for my telling her everything I know about teething, she will be able to elucidate the psychology of Biting Your Sister Because She Won't Play Pontoon.

She came home from her first lesson. 'I've got to find out what it really feels like to be a parent,' she said, 'but only with an egg.'

Here then is the plan. All students have to blow an egg, name it, draw a little face on it, and carry it with them everywhere for a week. If they want to play hockey they have to take it to the crèche, and if they want to go to a party they have to pay for an egg-sitter. Possibly the most inspired bit of teaching I've ever encountered.

So arrived Eggward, a lovely little free-ranger with no hair. At dinner there was no sign of him. 'He's having an early night,' explained the Senior

Daughter, only two hours a mother and already noticeably rattier.

Sad to say, Eggward was the victim of a careless playground accident at the tender age of three days. Was he dropped, or did he jump? We shall never know. Egglizabeth, a pale beige Size 2, Grade A, had replaced him within the hour.

Saturday came and the young mother wanted to go out and do her own thing. She didn't want to be seen in Top Shop with an egg. I said, 'I'd have loved to help. What a shame I'm too busy.' Then the Junior Aunt said she'd egg-sit for 25 pence an hour, payable in advance. I said, 'Take it! It's a steal! Do you have any idea what good childcare costs these days?'

How to prematurely age a fourteen-year-old. Take one egg . . .

GETTING THE MESSAGE

I've made a decision. From Monday, any child of mine coming in from school is going to be turned upside down at the door and shaken. The usual friendly greeting will also be available, and Standing Orders to remove anoraks before eating Penguins will remain in force. I merely want to get possession of any messages from school.

If Mrs Robinson has written to say please will I donate something for the Autumn Fayre, clearly I must be informed. Mrs Robinson's letter must be pressed firmly into hand. Then, if I get careless and forgetful and Mrs Robinson ends up with a tell-tale gap on the tombola stall, I shall have no one to blame but myself.

So there I was, staring gloomily into my early morning tea and wondering where flies go in winter, when the Middle Daughter, radiant for seven in the morning, said, 'Can I go then?' She had me lost. 'Can I go to Wembley to see the hockey?' she said, 'I gave you the letter about it.' Believe me when I tell you that she did not give me a letter about hockey at Wembley.

I'm not doubting that she brought that letter home. But at no time was it submitted through the proper channels. Neither was the one from Head of Music. More urgently, nor was the one about Harvest Festival. 'It's today,' said the Lad.

I suppose it's not much to ask of a woman. A bag of assorted groceries. A cheque for Wembley. A signed form for clarinet lessons. The Old Feller wandered through in optimistic pursuit of clean socks, and as we're an Equal Opportunities Family I tried a little buck-passing. 'Just make up a bag for Harvest Festival, would you,' I said casually, 'while I body-search this child for clarinet forms.'

'Certainly,' he said. 'Where's the bag? What do I put in it? Why do you make such a fuss about things? And has anyone washed any socks this week?'

It's probably this kind of reckless disregard for personal safety that makes men set off for the South Pole.

BROADCAST NEWS

I write in subdued mood this week. The biter bit.

The Senior Daughter has decided that the right of fair comment is as much hers as mine, that if a cap fits you should wear it, and that the broadcasting of juicy family secrets should not always be left to Weekend's 'Generation Games' correspondent.

'That's new,' she said, crawling from under my bed. 'Mind it doesn't get dusty while you're hiding it.' I waited for her to add, 'Just leave the money behind the pipes in the ladies' lavatory at Liverpool Street and your secret will be safe with me. Until the next time.' But that's not her style. She doesn't snoop for material gain. She's just a big mouth. I can see a terrific future for her when Nigel Dempster falls off his perch.

I love a good intrigue. Everyone I know has given up on ITV's mega-marathon Len Deighton serial, but I'm still with it, enjoying every bluff and counter-bluff, and wondering exactly how a woman with children could keep a job as a KGB agent.

If I can't stow away some modest purchase for five minutes without the town crier going about her business – 'Oyez! Oyez! Oyez! Laurie Graham bought two pairs of trousers! Hear all about it!' – what would be the chances of keeping a radio transmitter under wraps? Has Len really thought this through?

Meanwhile another little herald tribune is coming up through the ranks. 'Mummy got a new lipstick. And she said a rude word to the plumber.'

Here is the evening news; thirty seconds of reportage and incisive comment written and read by the Junior Daughter.

CURTAINS FOR SANTA

Christmas will be happening courtesy of Father this year. Father Graham, that is, not Father Christmas. Poor old Santa has been sent the buff envelope; he's been rumbled at last by the Junior Daughter.

'I nearly knew ages and ages ago,' she said, 'but last year there was a wasp in my stocking and it said Waitrose 50p, so then I really knew.' It was a

chocolate bee actually. Still, it was a careless slip. I don't suppose I'd make a very successful criminal.

'No point in hanging up our stockings then,' I said. No one agreed. The argument in favour of stockings ran roughly like this. Everyone likes stockings. Children like them full of comics and jelly beans. Daddies like them full of women. And Mummies are suckers for a nice little line of them hung from the mantelpiece. And since the unmasking of Santa has done nothing to change the identity of the actual filler of stockings, why tamper with tradition?

I only threw a small tantrum. I only tried to explain how much work goes into filling a stocking or four, but Father, in one of his egalitarian flushes, said, 'Quite right! Why should you do it all year after year. Leave it to me!'

I saw immediately that I was about to relinquish one of the very nicest duties of parenthood. 'It's all right,' I said. 'Stockings are an incredibly complicated skill, requiring the cunning of an adult and the mind of a child. You just deal with the food, the drink, the parcels, cards, crackers, over-excited children, offended aunts, and things made out of glittery pine cones, and leave the stockings to me.'

I still can't understand why he agreed. Hoping for a little Peace on Earth, possibly?

The Senior Daughter predicts he'll come in about 400 per cent over budget, but there will be savings. Such as Santa's double brandy. Personally I think he's doing a grand job. For a beginner.

NEARLY CHRISTMAS DAY IN THE COOKHOUSE

There is I suppose no greater challenge to the skills of motherhood than the three days before Christmas. School is out. The laundry basket is full of hockey socks last sighted in September. And each child has a wildly ambitious plan that involves glue, silver paper, and a strong hook in the ceiling.

This year the girls have decided to amuse themselves. They have learned that mothers with last-minute copy to file are best left out of anything to do with cardboard angels. But the Lad, ever optimistic, is in the mood to cook.

I sensed there might be something to my advantage in this. An easy escape from three dozen mince pies? A reprieve from cheese straws? 'These look fun,' I said. 'You just cut strips of pastry, twist an anchovy fillet round each one, and bake them in a hot oven.'

He didn't want to do that because he doesn't like anchovies. Not a particularly sound reason. I tried to seduce him with potato sticks. 'You just make a kind of dough with cooked potato and flour and things,' I said. 'Then you cut them into sticks, cover them with caraway seeds and cook them.' He didn't like the sound of that either. It was the caraway seeds that did it. We mothers can always tell.

'Okay,' I said, only very slightly desperate, 'Gingerbread Angels? Marzipan Fruits? Little stuffed thingummies made out of filo pastry?' All a waste of breath. What he wants to do to skip the years of sweat, tears, exhaustion and dismal failure and become the Roux brothers. Overnight. He wants to create *un Indulgent au chocolat*, which merely requires eight egg yolks, twelve ounces of *chocolat patissier*, a pint of cream, and a small bucket of Cointreau.

If it works out we may never eat Christmas pudding again. And if it doesn't, guess who will be hanging from that strong hook in the ceiling?

FOR LOVE AND MONEY

Everyone in our house got their Christmas wish this year. Some wanted knee-length red socks. Some longed for luscious *semillons* from the Barossa Valley. Some lusted after Electronic Blackjack. That's what makes the human race so fascinating.

Happiest by far was the Middle Daughter, and that was a very strange thing because she didn't actually get what she asked for. The Middle Daughter, as much in the mood to give as to receive, wanted to adopt an animal at London Zoo. Specifically, she wanted to adopt a penguin. Enquiries were made, and it turned out that this had been a terrific year to be a penguin. Penguins are all the rage.

I can remember polar bears being the thing round about 1955. I suppose puff adders keep wondering if their moment will come. Anyway, all the penguins were spoken for, and so were the suricate meerkats because they'd been on the telly behaving like absolute cards. I'm sure the grey seal population of the

North Sea would join me in observing that if you are a species at risk, it helps to be photogenic.

Our problem was, who to adopt? We could have had a water dragon for £15 a year. For £30 we could have kept a green acouchi or a stinkpot in whatever kind of hot dinners they prefer. We chose with a pin.

An Egyptian Vulture is a singular looking bird. Edith Sitwell, windswept, and without the jewels. I expect his mother loved him. The Middle Daughter certainly does and she plans to pay him a visit. But not before we have prepared her psychologically for an adoptee who shares her love of penguins, meerkats, voles, mice, fluffy bunnies, and even the blotched genet. Just as long as they come Ready to Serve.

COLD COMFORT

Certain members of the animal kingdom are able to maintain a constant body temperature irrespective of changes in their environment. Others are not so clever. These include fishes, reptiles and my four children.

In summer they suffered heat exhaustion and we had some very ugly scenes when there was a glitch in ice cube production. I even considered employing a part-time punkah wallah, but the weather broke before I could get down to the Job Centre to advertise.

Now we have winter. Are we down-hearted? Well

yes, we are a bit. We've plenty of woollies and Arctic-strength duvets. We've got open hearths, central heating and lagging in the loft. But it only has to drop a few degrees below freezing and I find myself whacking out bowls of porridge to the metabolically inert.

They lie in their beds whimpering. They cling to the radiators, wrapped in sleeping bags and bleat 'You'd never get away with this if we were in a union.'

Worst afflicted is the Heir Apparent. September to April he emerges from his pit like a constipated

lizard and looks wistfully at the thermostat. He wonders what life would be like in one of those families that gets up to a real fire and soft bath towels. I've told him. Hot is what it would be like. Hot and unhealthy.

Soft bath towels are one thing. Some day I may get round to providing them. But hot bedrooms are something else. They addle the brain, dehydrate the skin, and treble your gas bill. They don't do a lot for pluck and grit either. No wonder we lost the Empire.

January 1989

FIGHTING TALK

Hostilities have broken out again.

A childless guest, seated at our table, caught a whiff of grapeshot and asked, 'Do you ever feel you should intervene?'

A year ago I could have answered honestly that I did not. In the firm belief that everything except Ribena comes out in the wash, I've always let fights between children blow themselves out. If things threatened to escalate I had up my sleeve something smarter, cheaper and more easily deployed than Polaris. Me. One act of tyranny on my part, one high-handed edict, carefully selected to upset all four of them, and they forgot their quarrels to unite against the common enemy – Mother.

This isn't working any more. They've abandoned the trenches and taken to guerrilla warfare. They snipe from behind closed doors. And they have invented a hundred different ways to attack someone without moving an eyebrow.

'He called me a pig.'

'I never said a word.'

'He went oink-oink.'

'I didn't. That's the noise I make when I'm eating pickled onions.'

Here we had a situation that would tax the Secretary General of the United Nations. The Junior Daughter *is* especially sensitive to criticism. The Heir Apparent is *not* above the cunning use of

Noises Off. And pickled onions *were* being eaten. All this against a backdrop of the Middle Daughter, pockets full of bubble-gum wrappers, not being hungry for anything on her plate, and the Senior Daughter having trouble with catarrh.

Blessed are the peacemakers? Not necessarily. On this occasion, blessed is she who convicts on circumstantial evidence. Blessed is she who bans bubble-gum, sniffing at table, sister-baiting, and unauthorised use of pickles.

1989 – The Year of the Hawk. I never felt better.

February 1989

WORD PLAY

Laid up with the flu, I have been watching daytime television. I watched *Zig Zag's Wildlife Safari* and *Maths is Fun*, and then the Senior Daughter climbed into my bed and said, 'Feel my forehead. I think I've caught it. Don't you think I've caught it? Pass me the remote control pad please.'

I suggested we listen to the radio instead, but she said she had the sort of headache that gets worse if you listen to Poulenc too early in the day. I knew what she meant.

So we tuned to *The Pyramid Game*. A fast-moving quiz with contestants and celebrity guests, it said in the listings. I decided I'd risk its hectic pace even though I was supposed to be lying quietly, sipping iced water. I wanted to see what kind of person counts as a celebrity at 9.25 on a Thursday morning.

The Pyramid Game is a word game. One person tries to convey the meaning of a word and his partner has to name it. Someone should devise a more inventive version of it and call it Charades. I'm sure it'd catch on. Anyway, this tedious process of guessing four-letter words is made more exciting by the prospect of winning money. Spot enough words like *fork* or *vest* and you could leave the programme a couple of hundred smackers the richer.

'The next category is Astronomy,' said the quizmaster, and the studio audience shuddered. 'That's a long word,' he said. 'Sounds like I've swallowed a dictionary.'

But it isn't a long word, is it? It's shorter than *television*. And a lot shorter than *fantastically*, a word you hear all the time on quiz shows. It isn't even a difficult word. I said, 'Is that man being patronising or what?' And the Senior Daughter said, 'Patronising? That's a bit of a mouthful so early in the day. Let's see what time *Finger Mouse* is on.'

Words failed me.

1066 AND ALL THAT

The Battle of Hastings has been postponed. I'm not sorry. With the benefit of hindsight Harold would readily have admitted there's no sense getting into a scrap if you're tired and emotional.

The first I knew that the Normans were even thinking of invading was the Heir Apparent measuring a piece of dowelling on Monday afternoon. 'I'm a Norman,' he explained. 'I need a sword and a shield by Friday. And if there's enough left, can we make a sword for Gresham major. He's a Norman too.'

The Heir Apparent is an enterprising lad. He had already earmarked a piece of hardboard for his shield. The piece that usually stands behind his dart-board and stops the wall turning into a Gruyère cheese. 'You'll have to cut it into a kite shape,' he told me cheerfully. I already knew that. I'm not just a defroster of frozen pizza. I'm also a military historian.

What I'm not is a Master Armourer. Optimism and a fretsaw were clearly not going to get me very far. 'Wait till your father gets home,' I said, and his three sisters immediately hid in their rooms. They thought I'd said '*Just* wait till your father gets home.'

He said, 'I'm glad I'm a Norman. We win.' 'But do you know *why* you win?' I asked him. 'Because Mr Kinloch says we do.' While we waited for Father, I tried to shine a little light into the darker recesses of the Norman mind. 'Archers,' I said, 'and horses and stirrups. Where are the horses coming from?' He hadn't thought about horses.

So when it happens, this will be a Battle of Hastings with a twist. No cavalry. The rustics will look ugly with pitchfork and axe. The barons will look *chic* in denim and sneakers. But the outcome is anyone's guess. History may be rewritten.

Unless Gresham major would rather be a horse.

VICTORY AT LAST

Last Sunday the Heir Apparent stumbled upon a parent, head in hands, weeping 'It's no good. I can't go on.' Pieces of the Junior Daughter's Easy Assembly Doll's House lay all about. As did the glue, the paint, the sandpaper and a very full ashtray. 'Ah,' said the Lad. 'Glue! Can we make my ship?'

He's only had his scale model construction kit of H.M.S. *Victory* a year. Why are children so impatient?

Offhand I couldn't think of a reason not to make a start, so he lined up the little pots of paint, while I read that the use of tweezers was recommended for locating small parts, and that the gallant old lady of the sea has an extreme beam of 51 feet 10 inches. And I thought *I* needed more exercise!

'First,' I said, 'you're supposed to paint the cathead black, and the bitts and davits brown.' 'Do you mean buff?' he said. That boy never listens. It's the *bowsprit* you have to paint buff. Who ever heard of a buff davit?

The secret of success when you have 350 very small pieces of plastic is good organisation. You don't want forty gun covers cemented down when you might want to give the French fleet the impression that you're open for business, and you don't want anyone tampering with your shrouds. I said, 'Put the kettle on,' but he was itching for some action. And for some answers.

'The pointed end is the bow,' I explained, 'and the cathead sticks out of the pointed end so that the anchor ropes can feed through it. Lemon tea please.' 'Could this be it?' he asked, poking me in the eye with the mizzen mast.

So I told him the tale of Horatio Nelson. 'He lost an eye,' I said, 'then he lost an arm. His last order was *England expects every man this day to do his duty,* and when he caught it from a musket and lay dying in the cockpit of *Victory,* his final words were . . . that bulkhead should be blue, not gold and don't I get a biscuit?' Too early to splice the mainbrace.

SHORT CUTS

We're away for Easter this year. Last year the choc-olate egg situation got completely out of control and I still had midriff bulge at Halloween. I blame it all on Grandad. It was his chance remark that he had never had an Easter egg that set in motion a manic purchase of Thomas the Tank Engine confectionery.

This year we're heading someplace where they have sunshine, and no Easter bunnies.

The Senior Daughter has assembled her holiday wear with customary flair. The motif of her Spring Collection is the cut-off look. It's very cheap, and very simple. Anyone can do it. I'll tell you how.

First, you take a garment that no one else would be seen dead in. This can come from a thrift shop or the redundant end of your mother's wardrobe. 'Do you still want this incredibly old and nasty black dress that makes you look like an advert for dandruff shampoo?' she asked me, with the scissors in her hand. That's the vital second ingredient. A pair of sharp scissors.

Frankly, I was never going to wear that dress again. It had been love at first sight, and as is usual in these cases, I repented at leisure. Even with the shoulder pads removed, it didn't quite make it. I handed it over.

The cut-off look is achieved very quickly. One minute you have a knee-length dress, the next you have a tube of amputated material and a sort of very short shirt.

Father said, 'Haven't I seen this before? Didn't this used to be a wildly expensive jersey dress that your mother has only had for ten years?' The Senior Daughter put him right though. She explained what a saving she'd made, and what a sensation she's going to be on the Côte d'Azur.

I'm just wondering how I'd look in a tube. And can you get Creme Eggs in Cannes?

April 1989

QUALITY TIME

When I waved Goodbye to PAYE and set up my typewriter on the kitchen table, I decided my children should be the first to benefit from my being at home. 'When they come in from school,' I thought, 'I'll lay down my Tippex and talk to them. About the day they've had. And life in general.' My mind raced on, to the comforts of the hearth, a freshly-brewed pot of tea, and cakes, possibly home-made. The cake fantasy was symptomatic of how far I had wandered from reality.

But I was not alone. I got plenty of encouragement. Not least from Gran, who was always on hand in a clean pinny when I came home from school, and from my friend Sandra who once lived in America for five minutes and never lets anyone forget it.

'It's called Spending Quality Time with Your Kids,' said Sandra. 'It was a very big thing in Boston, Massachusetts. I've always made it a rule to be completely available to Tim and Sophie the moment school is out.'

I would have liked to ask whether she felt this was a contributory factor to Sophie and Tim growing up loud, rude and insufferably demanding, but politeness prevented me.

Sandra's lecture on the Theory and Practice of Quality Time was wasted on me anyway. My children rejected it as completely unnatural.

When *they* get in from school they need to drop

their coats on the floor, phone friends they haven't seen for half an hour, fight over the last Kit-Kat, watch *Jossy's Giants*, and then sit on the lavatory, singing tunelessly and forgetting what they went there for, until dinner is served. They tell me this is very therapeutic. That they wouldn't be nearly such nice people if they weren't left to coast mindlessly after a long hard day.

Sandra says they're just avoiding my Dundee cake.

TALKING SHOP

Shopping isn't what it used to be.

When I was a girl you went to M & S for your vests, Boots for bronchial mixture and Woolworth's for stick-on soles and broken biscuits. In 1955 would you have believed anyone who told you the day would come when you could buy a telephone from Woolies, a computer from Boots the Chemist, and champagne and squid from the vest shop?

The Junior Daughter is a heroic shopper. She may well mature into the kind of woman who goes on a daytrip to Boulogne and spends it searching for British Home Stores. Bad weather doesn't stop her. Neither does an income of five pounds a month.

When she got wind of a closing-down sale at a nearby costume jewellery shop, she was round there faster than you can say 'American Express'. Apparently they didn't have a lot left. No surprise this. They didn't have a lot to begin with. It was the kind of shop where they displayed three brooches inside a spotlit case and the salesgirls looked at you as though you'd trodden in something.

She came back with a pair of earrings that were absolutely *le dernier mot*. Two pairs for a pound but as there was only one pair left they'd given them away. A great bargain, even for a small girl who doesn't wear earrings.

Her next outing brought forth a heavily reduced 1989 diary and a job lot of synthetic bath sponges. 'Have a sponge,' she said. 'You can have pink, or another sort of pink.' Which cheered me up no end because I'd just been shopping too and I'd discovered that someone had beaten me to the last *Radio Times*, there was a city-wide shortage of black shoelaces, and that in Woolworth's, single purchases of more than one hundred red plastic noses must be referred to the store manager for authorisation.

Thwarted again.

SPORTING LIFE

The Heir Apparent could do with an early night. He's had a hectic couple of weeks, and staying up secretly and disobediently to watch greyhound racing from Catford never helped anyone to rise like a lark.

It all began when he was losing sleep over Ted Dexter. Was Ted about to name Gower as England captain for the full series, or merely for the first Test? Worse still, but the possibility had to be faced, was he going to name Gower at all? The tension was unbearable.

I have always taught my children that work is the best therapy for a troubled mind. 'Clean your shoes,' I suggested. 'Hang up your trousers.' But all he could do was rustle the pages of *Wisden* and look anxious.

When the news finally broke we were among the first to know. The Senior Daughter's newspaper round ensures we get the headlines, good or bad, very early. 'This is the best day of my life,' he said when we told him. I suppose Gower was pretty tickled about it too.

I thought he'd settle after that. I thought he'd watch *Sporting Triangles* and go to sleep like a good boy. But he didn't. Contrary to all good sense and threats of major surgery, he watched the feather-weight boxing and then those greyhounds. And when I went to wake him in the morning, was he spry and cheerful? Did he open his beady little eyes and say 'Good morning Mother! How are you on this beautiful spring day?' Or was he slothful and surly? Did he groan? Did he grunt? Is water wet?

Clearly the remedy is nine hours a night from now until *Test Match Special*. But he's already bunged in an appeal for the sentence to be suspended until after the World Snooker Championship.

I just hope David Gower is getting *his* jim-jams on nice and early.

FORMICA FOOD

Marseilles has to be one of the most challenging places in the world when you want a strawberry milkshake and a quarterpounder with cheese, easy on the gherkins. Not that Ronald McDonald hasn't arrived in that French stronghold of vice, corruption and fish-head soup. He's there, if you are desperate enough to seek him.

Gastronomically, our holiday was a limited success. In other respects my family took to France. They discovered it has a television channel devoted entirely to pop music, that Coca-Cola translates painlessly, and that when a nervous Gran meets a fully-automated music-while-you-work public lavatory you have pure theatre. 'Just put in your coin and the door will open.' 'Actually, I'm not particularly desperate. Maybe I could go behind that bush. Think of the saving!' Isn't it extraordinary? Just when you thought it was safe to trust French plumbing, along comes the space-age *sanisette*, specially designed to play on your most primitive fears.

They were not so entertained by the food.

I'm often told by other parents how their children have eaten their way across Europe. 'Harriet loved it!' they tell me. 'Lunchtimes we'd just fill a baguette with olives, goat's cheese, larks' tonsil pâté, and a little Lollo Rosso for that Continental touch, and she was good for another couple of hours looking at Romanesque churches.'

I'm baffled. When the children who like olives were being dished out, how come I didn't get one? How come I didn't even get one that likes tomatoes?

They won their war of attrition. I kept ordering fabulous grub. They kept leaving it. A broken woman, I agreed to a burger blow-out. It turned out to be a walk on the wild side. The Big M has set up shop along the more exotic stretch of red-light Marseilles and even on a Sunday afternoon trade was brisk. I expect the answer to 'Why is that man wearing a dress Mummy?' is 'Never mind about the man, eat up your cheeseburger,' whatever the language.

Then we came home. Sitting out an April blizzard in a motorway service station it was a relief to order three Porkie Platters and a Fillet of Haddock and know no one would grizzle. Maureen our waitress was proud to present a menu that did not involve olives, and the question before us was basically this – With chips, or without?

Maureen's perfume was more Hot Lard than *Ma Griffe,* and the passing cabaret lacked a certain raciness, but I comforted myself with the thought that 1992 isn't very many meals away. Anyone for an olive?

BIRDS OF A FEATHER

The delinquent blackbird has returned.

My understanding of blackbirds is that they wake at sunrise, spend the day in full-throated melodious song, and then shut up when it gets dark. Not this one. This one is fitted with a continuous-loop warning call.

The warning call of the blackbird is a kind of tchak-tchak-tchak, fired like a machine gun. Normal blackbirds use it to say 'Siamese Sealpoint at five o'clock and closing fast,' or 'The Robins have landed! Call out the Home Guard!'

Our blackbird uses the warning call to say 'The sun's shining. That *was* a nice slug. Anything for afters?' He also uses it at three in the morning. I think what he's saying then is 'Put that light out!' Imagine living with that when motherhood beckons.

They have moved into last year's nest. The hen arrived first, checked it for squatters and then signalled the All Clear. She spent half an hour bunging up a hole with mud and airing the beds, while he warned off the Old Feller's rugby shirt that was flapping with hostile intent on the washing line. By evening it was like they'd never been away.

We could tell when the eggs arrived. Suddenly he was doing the supermarket run on his own. He kept coming back with sirloin steak and Chocolate Chip ice-cream and we could hear her saying 'You've not forgotten the Duraglit *again*!'

She dropped in to see me after her confinement, but you don't get a lot of spare time with triplets. The little indicator that says This Blackbird is Empty keeps lighting up.

Mother Earth, Mother Nest, what's the difference? You incubate them, feed them, and the next thing you know they're off. They say they'll be home at six. By six thirty you're mad. By seven you're desperate. You scour the streets. Phone total strangers. You check the cupboards, fear the worst, and when you look out of the window what do you see?

The lost child. Hungry, grass-stained, ignorant of the time, oblivious of the twenty years he just added to your age, but found.

It's much the same with blackbirds. A triplet is easily mislaid once he's taken wing.

He thought it was great fun to swing from the Russian Vine whistling 'Look Mum, no claws!' while she cried 'Come down you foolish child. You're scarcely more than egg!' And Father manned the bren-gun. 'Colossal adolescent overhead! Action stations!' We call it Shared Parenting in our house.

May 1989

FLASHING THE FLAG

I didn't really want to go to Parents' Evening. It was the Old Feller who said I had to. 'Look upon it as a flag-flying exercise,' he said. But he hadn't seen our appointment schedule. I had.

8.20, Maths; 8.23, English; 8.26, Science; and on it rattled, like an American Tour of Europe. 'That's all right,' he said. 'We'll just hop from teacher to teacher.' Which just shows how little he knew, because Maths was in the East Wing and English was way out West. He'd barely have time to get that flag out of its paper bag.

I arrived at school in a pretty bad humour. What could anyone usefully say to me about my son in three minutes? That he is very able, very funny and bone idle? I already know. I live with him. That he draws terrific caricatures but has a lot of trouble with irregular verbs? I know that too. The Old Feller told me to stop snarling and look pleasant.

The system is that you queue. You do it right behind the parents who are currently having their three minutes' worth, thereby discouraging them from saying anything provocative or personal, except by special appointment in the Headmaster's Office.

Some teachers attract large crowds, and you have no way of identifying queue-jumpers or impostors. You don't take a numbered ticket like you do when you line up to buy salami. The best you can do is make a few tentative enquiries. 'Excuse me, are you History, 8.38?' 'No, we're actually Music, 8.56. We're just chatting to History, 8.41.'

Some teachers don't get a queue. They sit with their thermos flask waiting for Needlework, 9.17 and try to look cool.

After only three appointments we were running seriously late. The Old Feller didn't mind. He uses queues to adopt total strangers. 'Who was that?' 'No idea. Her husband's in Kuwait, her daughter's dyslexic, and she has a small mole on the inside of her right thigh.' But I minded. The caretaker was starting to stack chairs.

Why do caretakers do that? I do understand about overtime. I work a seventy-hour week myself. Overtime is written into my Life Plan. But I don't stack chairs when people are waiting for French, 9.23. And I don't sweep round their feet.

We never did see Geography. Her desk had been folded away. The caretaker, in drip-dry pyjamas and a striped towelling wrap showed us the door. I gave him E for Effort. He gave me A for Aggravation.

LOSS LEADERS

The Rule of Three has always interested me.

When I was a girl, if the milk went sour and the handle came off a cup, the family would prepare itself for the inevitable third mishap. 'There!' my Gran would say, with manifest relief, 'Your Grandad's done his thumb on the corned beef tin, so that makes three!' Then there'd be rejoicing by everyone except Grandad, who was looking peaky with a tea towel wrapped round his hand, and we all felt safe to go out and walk under ladders. I can't remember whether good things came in threes. Probably not.

But in our house good things *leave* in threes. First, the Heir Apparent's anorak. It was warm, it was showerproof, and it was a lovely shade of blue. One moment it was there, hung across the back of his chair in Maths, and the next moment . . . well, several hours later actually, it was gone. We looked upon it as a temporary loss. After all, it did have his name in it. It was clearly a question of waiting.

But the more we waited the more it didn't turn up. The Lad went to school in a spare anorak that was tailored for Guy the Gorilla. We'd only kept it for emergencies, but when an emergency happens, a magenta duvet with sleeves that touch knee-level doesn't really help you to cope.

The Middle Daughter was next. 'Don't shout,' she said, 'I left my plimmies on the bus.' 'Why weren't they in the proper bag,' I asked her, 'with your shorts, and your tracksuit?' I was very calm. I think the yoga is starting to work. 'They *were* in the bag with my shorts,' she said, feeding me the bad news piecemeal. 'I've left *everything* on the bus.'

It's a long way to the bus depot. You catch a Number 3 and then about half an hour after the last of the other passengers has alighted the driver turns to you and says, 'You look grim. Are you on your way to file a complaint?'

'I might be,' I said, 'if they haven't got a grey rucksack containing compacted sportswear,' and he smiled, because he knew and I didn't that they had a whole warehouse full of grey rucksacks, and none of them smelled very nice.

Two down, one to go. The Middle Daughter, again. She sat on my lap. She hugged me. 'It must be bad,' I thought. It was. 'You're going to go absolutely mad,' she said. I did.

A bus pass isn't a big thing to lose. Just very expensive and very inconvenient. Still, that did make three. We were due for a change. Like having our bike stolen.

The cosmic Rule of Three doesn't seem to be working any more. I think it may be getting blocked by all that intergalactic hardware. And microwave ovens probably don't help.

June 1989

JOBS FOR THE GIRLS

I've been trying to remember when Careers teachers were invented. In my day the options were clearly visible. If you were a girl you could become a teacher, a shorthand typist, or a nurse. Failing those three, you could spend two years on the Stick-On Soles counter in Woolworth's and then retire to early motherhood. If you were a boy you could become absolutely anything. Except a nurse.

We did have a Careers Advisory Service. It was the Chemistry master and a booklet called *So You Want To Be An Engineer?* But at least Engineering was something we could relate to. We could go to Open Day at the steam turbine factory and think 'Maybe I'd be happier in Soft Furnishings.'

What do today's Careers teachers say? How do you begin to explain Operations Management, or Corporate Psychology? What exactly does a Sector Analyst do? Or a Quality Assurance Technical Support Officer? And if you would ultimately like to earn 50K a year marketing a unique communications concept for a blue-chip company advantageously situated in the M4 corridor, is a year slicing bacon on YTS going to have been a wise step, or merely better than a poke in the eye?

The Junior Daughter said, 'What job do you do Daddy?' So he told her, but she didn't really understand. She's grown up with Postman Pat and the Trumpton Fire Brigade. I can see her problem.

I knew what my Daddy did, because his glasses were always speckled with white emulsion and he had a large following of middle-aged groupies whose husbands couldn't hang wallpaper. And the Old Feller knew what his Daddy did because he used to go down to Princes Street station and proudly watch him bring home the King's Cross train.

He said, 'Well sometimes I tell other people what to do and sometimes they tell me what to do. Sometimes we realise something needed doing and nobody did it. That's when we all go to the Beefeater and have a plate of chips and a good cry.' But she still wasn't sure.

She said, 'I don't think you're A Boss because if you were you wouldn't have to go to work on a nice day. You could take me swimming instead. I think,' she said, 'you are a sort of Decider. I think you have to open lots of bottles of wine and spit them out if they're nasty.' She wasn't wrong.

What she wants to know now is, how you become a Wine Spitting Decider. Me too.

NO SWEAT

We're just back from Paris, me and the Senior Daughter. Finishing her education? Barely starting it, my dears, barely starting it.

I made her sit through Mass in the cathedral of Notre Dame, where the music is sublime and the human traffic is a match for Oxford Street at the start of the January Sales. I made her eat a triple cornet on the Île St Louis, climb the Butte, ride the Pompidou escalator, and schlepp around Galeries Lafayette in search of a navy handbag. 'But Mum,' she said, 'they must have ten thousand navy handbags in here.' And so they had. They just didn't have quite what I was looking for. I exhausted the child.

For her the highlight of the trip was the two hours we spent doing nothing. The fact that we were going to have to do nothing stark naked in the rue Geoffroy-Saint-Hilaire was something I kept from her until we had reached the point of no return. Forewarned, there was a good chance she would have jibbed.

'This,' I told her 'is a mosque. Here is the courtyard. Here is a tea room. And here,' I said, pushing her through the hanging Axminster very fast, 'is the hammam. We're going to have a steam bath.'

This was an extraordinary culture shock for a modern Western girl. For all their liberties, she and her friends never spend time closeted from men, sipping mint tea and scrubbing each other's backs. We lay on our towels and tried to look like we did this kind of thing every Saturday. But the word had already gone round. 'English. The kind that steep themselves in dirty bathwater and call it cleanliness.'

In the First Steam Room the Senior Daughter's catarrh disappeared, and so did my mascara. In the Second Steam Room we dissolved. I suppose we should have been out there, beating the bicentenary bush for latex masks of Robespierre and digital guillotines, but it was much nicer to be sweating on a marble slab while the regulars compared husbands and stretchmarks.

We moved on to the masseuse. '*Regardez*!' she said, and with a sort of Brillo mitten began to scrub away at forty-two years' accumulated grime. She told me she loves her work. She likes the steam. She likes the way people talk to her. She's Claire Rayner in a swimsuit, and she gets all the mint tea she can drink.

We'll certainly be going back. Madame la Masseuse has shed a completely new light on A Dirty Weekend in Paris.

THAT OLD BLACK MAGIC

I should like to report an outbreak of paranormal happenings.

Something, or perhaps I should say Some Thing, for who can tell where it has come from or what its terrible mission may be, has been in my box of chocolates and eaten the soft centres.

Mothers nationwide will now be saying, 'So? Children buy you chocolates and then leave you the Praline Cracknels. What's new?' But this was different. These were very special chocolates.

I've been having a bit of trouble with my eyes. A temporary condition, luckily for me, but I haven't felt able to get out and about. 'You are a poor wreck,' said the Old Feller, always ready with a cheery word, and he went out and bought me those chocolates.

I took out my magnifying glass and read the little map in the top of the box. No Strawberry Creme.

No Turkish Delight. These were proper grown-up chocolates for a proper grown-up person, and there would be no point in anyone harassing me to swop my Vanilla Fudge for their half-eaten Montelimar because there weren't any. I was confident that no one would be tempted by chocolates with names like Sirene and Gianduja. I nibbled on a White Versailles and was a happy woman.

Next time I looked there was a space where there shouldn't have been. A Kirsch-flavoured cream with chopped cherries coated in finest Belgian chocolate had upped and gone.

'Okay,' I said, 'I suppose the red foil wrapper was

a dead giveaway. Who had it?' No one. The Junior Daughter had a suggestion though. 'Perhaps it was a mouse,' she ventured. 'Perhaps it crept in from the garden and secretly ate it.' And everyone agreed that that was the most likely explanation.

It wasn't until the next day, when I thought I might toy with a Fleur-de-Lys that I discovered I was missing two Tiffanies and half of a Nelson. That mouse had evidently found the Cognac filling too heady, and left it in a slobbery heap.

This was really too much. I called an Extraordinary Family Meeting. 'I wouldn't have minded,' I told them, feigning more sorrow than anger, 'but look what you've left me. Praline with Puffed Rice, Orange Praline, Praline with Orange Flavour, or Praline with Added Praline. Own up!' I begged them. 'Raise your hand whoever it is that hates Praline, and that'll make two of us.' But nobody did.

'Perhaps,' said the Junior Daughter 'a robber came. Perhaps he knew you can't see very well this week.'

She may be right. But I must warn him. The eyes in the back of my head are in perfect working order.

EDUCATING ARCHIE

Six months have passed since the Middle Daughter adopted an Egyptian Vulture. She thought it really was time we visited him, and though I'm no great lover of zoos I had to agree. We pencilled in Tuesday for dropping in on Archie.

The secret with zoos is self-discipline. You've got to make a list of what you want to see, then halve it. And you've got to check out those special events *before* you get sidetracked by moulting camels. If you don't, you might miss Rosie the Rhino practising for Elementary Charging and Butting Grade I.

The Junior Daughter wanted to see rabbits and pigs, and Gran wanted to see lions. But first things first. We were there to visit family.

I asked the girl who was cleaning out the owls. 'Vultures?' she said, evidently baffled by people who want to look at anything but owls. 'I should try with the pheasants.' So we did, but he wasn't there. The lady in the Information Kiosk thought he might be with the cranes. He wasn't, but I was grateful to her for her suggestion because without it I'd never have discovered that a crane can do a pretty good impersonation of Max Wall. Perhaps I'll adopt one. Perhaps I'll adopt Max Wall.

'Excuse me,' I said to a man being walked by an elephant, 'Do you know where I'd find an Egyptian Vulture?' 'Certainly,' he said. 'Turn right at the Conveniences, and head towards the eagles.' And sure enough, that's where we found him.

The excitement of being face to face with her adopted grand-vulture proved too much for Gran. 'Come down off your perch!' she called, and when he wouldn't she climbed on a bench and took a photograph of his parson's nose. This is how the vandal element of Senior Citizen Bus Pass-holders carries on after one bag of crinkle-cut crisps and a swig of lukewarm Chardonnay. We made her get down off the bench and took her to see Life with the Lions.

Unfortunately the lions were busy being lions. A squirrel had chanced his luck once too often and was about to become a mid-afternoon snack. A nice reminder, this, of the natural scheme of things. We hurried along to see our old friend Taff the Pony Who Bites. He lives next door to the Goats Who Eat Everything. Except that they don't. They don't eat small boys called Ryan who drop sweet wrappers on the ground, more's the pity.

Then we gave Archie a second chance. We sat quietly by his cage and hoped he might turn round. Nothing doing. The raven next door was busy strutting his stuff, but not Archie. Of course, he's young yet. Still learning about show business.

PROBLEM PARENTS

I was interested to learn from my Sunday newspaper that bringing up children is a long and complicated job for which many of us are ill-prepared and in need of expert advice.

The Parent Network runs nationwide twelve-session courses in basic parenting. The Network's starting point is that if we adopt the methods of child-rearing our parents used we shall come to grief. 'The world has changed,' they tell us, 'and hardly any of the old rules still apply.' Haven't they got that the wrong way round? Isn't the problem that the old rules do still apply but no one can be bothered to use them?

Now for a much heavier scene. *Exploring Parenthood* is also a charity, funded in part by the Department of Health. EP runs stress workshops for parents like Diane, a mature woman with two children, a busy husband and a problem. According to Diane her way of life has changed. She and her husband used to go out together, and entertain. Now she finds restrictions on her independence, tension in her marriage and I suspect, though she doesn't say it, roller skates on the stairs and Farex on her trousers. What I haven't been able to work out is, precisely what is her problem?

If she's saying that sitting at home with two cases of chicken-pox and a dog-eared edition of *Rumpelstiltskin* is not her idea of fun, I have to agree with her. If she's saying that fathers should do more than buy train sets and snarl from deep armchairs, I'm with her there too. But I still can't see a problem.

Diane isn't living in a Bed & Breakfast. She has her health, and her husband and children have theirs. And as she's resident in the United Kingdom she's not significantly at risk from mud slides or locust plagues. In fact I'd say that on the global scale of disease, hunger and hopelessness Diane was doing quite nicely.

Still, she's clearly not happy. She's discovered the hidden agenda of parenthood. That small children run off with your vigour, your looks, and your money, at the same time pocketing your scissors and your Sellotape, and that all they give you in return is indiscriminate, unconditional love.

I've got news for Diane. It gets worse. The day-light robbery continues, but the claw-back diminishes. How can they possibly love you when you make them wear an anorak *with an elasticated waist*! And how can you say you love them but not let them watch *Prisoner:Cell Block H*?

But it's the Sellotape situation that really gets me down. Do you think I need therapy?

SALAD DAYS

When is a Spring Roll not a Spring Roll? And under what circumstances does a Waldorf Salad cease to be?

No philosophical stroll, this. I am talking Empty Larder. The bottom line here is Ingredients.

The Heir Apparent has been doing cookery at school this year. It appears on his timetable as Home Economics – a misnomer if ever there was one. I'm glad to say he's about to hang up his apron and learn German, which will be easier on my budget and jolly useful when we become a small island off the coast of Euroland.

'Tomorrow I'm making Spring Rolls,' he said. I told him the bad news immediately. 'I'm afraid you're mistaken,' I said. 'If only you'd warned me, I'd have made sure we had everything you needed.' But he wasn't so easily defeated. 'We've got flour,' he said, 'and eggs, milk, salt, pepper, and onion. Where do we keep the bean sprouts?' Even when it dawned on him that we were fresh out of bean sprouts, even when I'd convinced him that I did not have a red pepper concealed about my person, he still wouldn't surrender. 'I'll put grated cheese in them instead,' he said, and disappeared out of the door with a piece of Mature Mousetrap in his satchel.

The Spring Rolls didn't really work out. In fact they were so dismal he dumped them in a litter bin on the way home and I had to comfort myself with the thought that he had at least learned the importance of planning ahead, and of improvising only when you have a very sure touch.

'I can't find any walnut halves,' he said at five o'clock on Wednesday evening. I explained that I don't care much for walnuts, and he explained how walnuts are a *sine qua non* for Waldorf Salad. And so is celery, which I don't like either. 'Make it without walnuts and celery,' I suggested, performing a shameless U-turn. 'Make it with cashews!' But he sighed and set off for the supermarket with a shopping list clutched in his hot little hand.

He made that Waldorf Salad, correct in every detail. He carried it home tenderly, protecting it from the ravages of Nasty Norman's bus driving, transferred it to a china dish, garnished it with a little extra apple, and asked me what I thought.

What I thought was, I didn't want to eat it. What I thought was, what's with all this slavish conformity to the recipe? Since when do teenage boys heed motherly advice? And is it possible that one bad do with a Spring Roll has scarred him for life?

WINNING INNINGS

In the matter of my son's sporting life I've always taken a back seat. I'm entirely in favour of sport, for those gifted enough to be able to make hand, ball and eye connect, but my understanding is flimsy, and my enthusiasm has never been warmer than tepid. My role has been to stick plasters on sore heels, and dispose of shower towels that have entered an advanced stage of decomposition.

So last Sunday when the Lad was called up to play for The Casuals, I went through my usual routine – 'Have you whitened your pads, packed your sun hat, and done something with that piece of twine that's been dangling from your bat handle for ever?' – and then retired to the kitchen to do something brave with a leg of lamb.

During the afternoon the Old Feller strolled over to the ground, looked at the scorecard and strolled back again. 'Hold the fancy cooking!' he said, 'this is England, the sun's shining, and your son just made eleven runs. Now come and watch him field.'

I didn't really want to. I felt that sitting on the pavilion steps with self-raising flour in my hair I might jinx his performance. We concealed ourselves behind a tree, and by peering round it very discreetly I was able to work out that when he wasn't fielding at deep mid-on he was fielding very aptly at silly point, and that the batsmen were both built like brick outhouses.

Then, something quite unforeseen. He was asked to bowl. I couldn't watch. How could I watch? 'Have the game stopped!' I said to the Old Feller. 'He's too young to get hit all over East Anglia! I only potty-trained him ten years ago!'

He bowled six overs and I spent them all with my eyes shut. Well, I did have a quick squint at one delivery, and he did bowl a nice line and length, but of his three maidens, four byes, a wide and *five wickets for three*, I saw nothing but the inside of my eyelids.

Time then to reflect that a hundred years ago he'd have been old enough to work down the pit, and in 1914 he could have been one of those who fibbed and volunteered for Flanders. Time to reflect that on a different toss of the coin, in 1989 he might be out on the streets of Beirut or Belfast. He might be one of El Salvador's *perdidos* or relishing his golden youth from the pointed end of *intifada*.

Yet another reminder that he's a very lucky little

bowler. And that for many thirteen-year-old boys, life isn't really cricket.

GOOD WORDS

The Senior Daughter has just finished a week of Work Experience. One of the benefits of being a fifteen-year-old in 1989 is that you get the opportunity, local labour market permitting, to taste the world of work before you are obliged to chew it up and swallow it.

The process started months ago when, with one eye on a career backstage, she asked a local theatre if they would give her a week's work. That was when I discovered that she was full of initiative and drive, but did not know how to write a proper letter. I was happy to make good the deficiency. I felt I shouldn't have needed to, but I was willing to help.

Last Monday morning her initiative and drive had deserted her. So had her courage. She put her head under her pillow and said she didn't want to learn how to light a stage. She wanted to stay home with me and do colouring in. But I was horrible to her. I even made her eat breakfast. Monday evening she crawled home. She was very dirty, she knew how to assemble the kitchen table for Act I of *Shirley Valentine*, and courtesy of Mr Shifter and his band of merry men she had doubled her knowledge of Anglo-Saxon. 'So you're happy to go back tomorrow morning?' I asked her. But she was asleep.

Tuesday she came home with a mild case of Keyboard Shoulder. 'I've been in the same position *all day!*' she told us. 'We're doing a publicity mailshot and I've been sitting in front of a word processor for hours!' This was terrific. She was gaining an insight into High-Tec Neck Pain and she was learning jargon. 'Lining up the dolly is harder than it looks,' she said with throwaway ease. 'Is my jumper clean for the morning?'

The down side of this story is that many of the Senior Daughter's classmates stayed in the classroom and they needn't have done. They are growing up in an area of high employment. Local businesses had offered work. We can't all be self-starters, but those who were invited to take up one of those Work Experience opportunities but not pressed, by parents or school, to accept, missed something of very great value.

We sneaked in to have a look at her on her last night. She was on Programmes and Ice-Creams, smiling pleasantly at the punters and giving them the right change. 'I could see you,' she said, when we met her at the Stage Door long after her bedtime and ours, 'I could see you down in Row G, pretending not to be there. I wish I could come back for another week.'

I wish she could too. I never saw anyone grow up with such speed and such good humour. But for now, back to the classroom.

August 1989

FAMILY PENANCE

The Home Secretary has recently proposed that magistrates should have the power to penalise the parents of juvenile offenders. My gut reaction to this news, as the parent of juveniles who, so far, are non-offenders, was approval. It also reminded me of an incident that gave me a taste of what it might be like to have a delinquent in the family.

Some years ago, one of my children, hereinafter referred to as It because It has paid Its debt to society and doesn't deserve a Grub Street exposé, wandered from the straight and narrow whilst riding Its bike and scratched the paintwork on a neighbour's car.

It came straight home and owned up. Probably because the neighbour was already on his way round with steam coming out of his ears. The matter was quickly resolved. Parents and child apologised and the aggrieved party was invited to send us the bill, with half of the repair costs to be met by the child Itself.

The next day I told the tale to a colleague – a man who had reared three daughters to exemplary adulthood. He was appalled. First, that I should expect my child to contribute to the bill. Second, and worse, that I was willing, in fact eager, to discuss the episode publicly. In his view I should have paid up and guarded the shameful family secret with my life. I thought he was wrong and I still do.

The damage my child had done was negligent, not malicious. Nevertheless I felt ashamed, discredited as a mother, and in urgent need of catharsis. Our little act of united family penance made me feel a lot better.

Of course, Douglas Hurd's new policy is not about restoring parents' self-esteem. It's about deterrence and reformation. Most adult criminals start their careers as juveniles. In 1987, 6000 crimes were committed by children under the age of criminal responsibility, and there is scant hope that the figures for 1988 will be any lower. And yet a criticism already made of the proposed new powers is that a criminal court is not the appropriate arena for examining parental responsibilities.

Criminal courts are intimidating places. Even in the public gallery, the ritual formality never fails to deliver the message that crime is serious. That's the whole point of it. That's what makes it *exactly* the right place to confront parents with the consequences of their child's behaviour.

I've long since forgotten how much that bill was. But the sight of a white Ford Escort still makes me blush to the roots of my hair.

HOOFERS

We went to Newmarket, the Old Feller, the Middle Daughter, and I. The sun was shining, we hadn't been for a week or three, and so we thought 'Why not?'

But this was to be no ordinary day's racing. I was first alerted to this fact by the sight of a monstrous, inflatable presence bobbing silently in the Suffolk sky. Was it Sheikh Mohammed, dropping in by dirigible so as to give his Cessna the weekend off? Was it a Channel 4 anchorperson who had stumbled on the secret of human flight? Neither. It was a Hot Air Kiwi.

I needed no further clues. This was New Zealand Day – not, please note, Waitangi Day which is February 6th and which next year will mark the 150th anniversary of the signing of a bit of paper by the natives who had been there from approximately the dawn of time and the British who were out for a Sunday drive.

I know all this because the New Zealand High Commissioner stood on Newmarket Heath and told us so. But I run ahead of myself.

I bought a race card. It should have had a picture of a horse on the front. Who ever heard of a race card with a bird on the cover? But apparently Kotuku the White Heron is very big with the Maoris, and on these occasions one defers to one's guests.

We avoided the Jockey Club canteen. I couldn't bear to contemplate what extra uses they might have found for thinly-sliced kiwi fruit. We lunched outside with good old British wasps for company, and I had just settled down to mark my card when we were summoned to the finishing post for a display of Maori dancing. The Middle Daughter wouldn't hear of missing it.

They were a handsome bunch, in classic black and white, cleverly accessorised with volcanic mud. Like Greek folk songs, their dances took ten minutes to explain and one minute to perform, and the gist of them all was that big trees are awe-inspiring and colonialism stinks.

I said, 'I think we've seen enough of this,' but the Middle Daughter wanted to stay to the end. They'd just finished one with arm movements which translate into modern English as 'Oh you careless driver you!' and were about to do one expressing Maori aspirations. But I had aspirations myself. In the Maiden Stakes due off at 2 o'clock.

The Middle Daughter put me straight. 'You go to the Tote,' she said, 'I'll stay here. And does Daddy know there are men in the Members' Enclosure wearing bath towels and no tie?'

I would have said she's become a woman of the world. If only she knew where New Zealand is.

PLUMB WRONG

Earlier this week I received a newspaper cutting. Just another story about a tiny village school that is about to bite the dust. Its children and parents, passionate about keeping the school open, half-crazy with frustration and impotence, had taken their campaign to Westminster, and the saga was of interest to me because ten years ago that same little school was under threat of closure, and I was one of the embattled parents.

I suppose we should hold one minute's silence for the bean-counters at County Hall. They're not made of money. But it is sometimes worth asking why they think they need to be.

The school in question is virtually all that remains of a village that once truly lived. One pub, one shop, a church but no resident vicar, and a bus that runs sometimes. But the heart is still beating. The school has twenty-six pupils, aged five to seven, and a light, pleasant Victorian classroom. It is substandard. The incredible figure of £100,000 has been quoted for bringing it up to par, quite a bit of it to correct a grave deficiency. This is a school with Outside Lavatories.

I grew up with outside toilets. My grandparents

never used anything else. Even when the social climbers in the family started converting broom cupboards, my grandmother still preferred the sound of birdsong and the wind gusting round her ankles. My father was personally responsible for the creation of our own In House Facilities, but he never threw off his own habit of Going Outside. There was no lock on the door. He whistled so everyone knew he was in there, and it was there that he did his finest thinking.

He wasn't the only one. Uncle Jim enjoyed the benefit of semi-detached earth closets. He could do what a man had to do, and sometimes do it in company. One day, words with Nev on the curse of blackfly, the next – because Nev wasn't a man of such regular habits – solitary contemplation amongst the dead leaves and spiders. Just like Martin Luther, who was a martyr to his bowels. It's worth considering that if the plumbing had been more opulent in sixteenth-century Wittenberg we might never have had the Reformation.

More pressingly, it's worth considering every possible economy to preserve our village schools. No one learns less seated at an old desk. Central heating doesn't increase intellectual vigour. In fact doesn't fresh air clear the head and concentrate the mind? Perhaps we should make the School Provision Panel Go Outside and see?

THE INCREDIBLE BULK

Last Saturday as we got in line for the slowest super-market checker known to humankind I saw a face I recognised. 'The chap with two pineapples and nothing else,' I whispered to the Old Feller, 'why do I know him?' but he couldn't help me. He was wrestling with one of those trolleys that has four left wheels.

Was it the man who fixed our ballcock? Was it Clive James? I remembered. He and I had both been guests at an elegant dinner. I'd worn something brave in black Lycra and been full of the sort of wit brought on by two dry sherries. Now here I was with a truck full of Monster Munchies, my credibility as a sophisticate utterly blown.

'My word!' he said, ogling all our grub, 'do you run a hotel?' I explained to him that this was what it took to keep four growing children in hot dinners and clean shirts for just one week.

I felt exposed by his interest in what we were buying. I tried to shuffle a few green vegetables to the top of the heap, and wished I didn't have quite so many white sliced loaves. But I had no right to any privacy. I've peered into other people's baskets for years, trying to imagine what anyone would do with seven tins of processed peas. And my recent researches in the *Euro-Monitor* have provided me with some fascinating glimpses of consumer passions.

You probably already heard that we head the European league table for toilet soap sales and the French bring up the rear, covering the smell of Gallic sweat with their phenomenal purchases of perfume. But did you know that West Germany buys the most fabric conditioner? And Italy the most washing-up liquid? Did you know that for expenditure on pan scourers and Vim we are neck-and-neck with Denmark for first place?

In the matter of breakfast cereal that goes snap, crackle, toilet paper that does not, and pizza fashioned in the form of Brontosaurus Feet, I could find no statistics, but I have a feeling my family is up there with the big boys. And if not for those items, then for their heroic consumption of Plough-man's Pickle and those sublime iced lollies that have nutty bits on the outside and chocolate in the middle.

Yet we Brits are reckoned to be the cheese-parers of Europe. The supermarket meanies with sweet-smelling armpits. As a nation we spend a measly 14 per cent of our disposable income on food.

I couldn't believe this, so I've done a few sums and I've come to the conclusion that I'm picking up someone else's 14 per cent as well as my own. Prob-ably Pineapple Pete's.

September 1989

AN EYE FULL OF SOAP

I suppose school holidays wouldn't be school holidays without me blasting into orbit over the number of hours spent in front of the television. A long, hot summer? Certainly. You could fry an egg on the top of our set.

Mainly they have been watching Australian soaps. Any spare time has been spent watching repeats of Australian soaps.

I should begin by saying that my attitude to soap operas has always been tolerant. They seem to me to strike exactly the right note for the televisual medium – trivial, harmless and quickly forgotten. I'm a veteran follower of *Coronation Street*, and a latecomer, but a devoted one, to *EastEnders*. These days, when I find most television irksome and unsatisfying, they are pretty well the only programmes I watch.

The traditional television dispute between parents and children runs as follows: 'Why don't you switch that off and do something?' 'Can we go skating/rowing/water-skiing/shopping in Hamley's with a blank cheque?' 'No.' 'In that case can we have the television back on?' 'All right. But for goodness sake watch something *educational*.'

Parents, who dearly wish they had more time for brass-rubbing and building tree-houses, are grateful for something that keeps children silent and stationary for £67 a year, and which promises occasionally to educate and inform. But here is where I fall out with television. Its power to educate and inform is vastly overstated. It promises what it cannot deliver, and we're all so comfortable in our armchairs we don't complain.

Television shows us what is televisible. It takes a subject with programme potential, carves it and bones it into micro-portions and gussies it up with some sexy graphics. It rarely gives us anything raw to get our teeth into, because it's so very expert at chewing our food for us. And if a subject doesn't have camera appeal it might as well not exist.

I tried to make this point to the Senior Daughter. I said, 'Do you ever stop to think how television distorts your view of the world? Do you ever worry about the millions of things that are happening Off Camera?' 'No,' she said, 'not as long as I can watch *Neighbours*. What I worry about is having a mother who still watches *Sesame Street*.'

But who could resist? Yo-Yo Ma and the Sesame Street Gang playing Beethoven's Quartet for cello, two honkers and a dinger. Murray van Beethoven, I believe. *That's* what I call worthwhile television.

REGULATION BLUES

Last week, when desperate women nationwide were pounding the streets in search of navy serge, I found myself with uncommonly little to do. For the first time in years only two of my children will be wearing school uniform.

The Senior Daughter is now old enough for the privilege of wearing her own choice of clothes at school. This is supposed to make you feel less confined by pre-historic arbiters of fashion, and open up exciting new arenas of self-expression. But not when your mother is a stodgy old buffer like me.

All I have asked of the girl is that she chooses something comfortable and machine-washable, and then addresses her mind to her GCSEs. My case wasn't helped by a recent colour supplement feature on *What Sixth Formers Are Wearing This Year*. It isn't inevitable that an obsession with fashion signals a generally silly attitude to life, but complementary pieces on what Sixth Formers are thinking, doing and reading would have gone some way to reassure me.

Like many fifteen-year-olds the Senior Daughter knows she wants to make a statement about herself. That's as far as she's got. I said, 'While you're working out what you want to say to the world, what's wrong with a nice woollen jersey?' '*Nice* is what's wrong with it,' she barked. And garment by garment we worked our way through every twentieth-century totem of badness and rebellion.

'Denims?' 'That depends,' I told her. 'There are denims, and there are denims.' 'Leather jacket?' she said, raising the stakes out of sight. 'Definitely not,' I replied. 'a) you're too young to go round looking so mean and cool, b) it'll get stolen and c) you said I could have a turn at wearing it this winter.' Depression set in.

I tried to jolly her out of it with tales of my youth. I told her about my run-in with authority over starched petticoats. How the world went mad in 1959 and our underskirts got bigger and crunchier by the hour. Some of us were made examples of in front of the whole school, and my heroine, The Wickedest Girl In The School, was gated for a week for defiantly wearing four layers of froth. This ripping yarn cut no ice with the Senior Daughter. She wanted action.

The terms of our truce have allowed some progress. She's agreed to stop toying with the Gothic Horror Look. I've agreed to stop banging on about quality and cut. You have to get these things in perspective. After all, The Wickedest Girl In The School will now be nudging fifty.

WRITEFUL PLACE

Twenty years ago, when I read Virginia Woolf more for effect than pleasure, I came across her thoughts on the practical difficulties of being a female writer. Not a woman to have spent much time at the mangle herself, she drew a sharp enough picture of lives consumed with exhaustion and interruption, where only the childless and the seriously rich had a hope in hell. 'If a woman is to write,' said Mrs W, 'she must have money and a room of her own.'

I ignored her advice and wrote my first book on the corner of a table used for eating dinner and building Lego castles. Whether I failed to produce a work of genius because my imagination faltered, or because someone put Hubba-Bubba on my typewriter bail bar, we shall never know. The world continued to roller skate around me and I pressed on with several more books.

Now things have changed. I warned them they would. Now I have a room. It has a desk, and a chair, and a bird's-eye view of my neighbour's fig tree. What more could I possibly need? A waste-paper bin? A padlocked box of Black Cherry Sponge Thins? Or a bit of technology to bring me up to speed?

Cutting a deadline excitingly close the other day, I got a call from the editor. 'Laurie,' she said, 'we look forward to receiving your piece soonest.' *Soonest* is a recent and ugly fast-lane invention. It means 'We wanted it yesterday.' I explained that I'd all but finished and would be nipping it round to the pillar-box within the hour. 'Fax it,' she said. 'You do have a Fax?'

I swung round in my swingaround chair. I did not have a Fax machine. And if someone had knocked at my door and said 'Have a Fax. We're giving them away,' it's hard to say where I'd put it, what with the laundry basket and the permanently erected ironing board, the suitcase of things that would only take someone five minutes to repair, and the sagging but immensely useful old settee.

The Junior Daughter likes to collapse on it and petition for a hamster. The Middle Daughter favours it for Science homework. And the Heir Apparent swears there's no better place for kicking off your shoes, loosening your tie, and preventing your mother from earning a living. I like to think Mrs

Woolf would have seen the point of my settee. Especially when I rifle it for coins of the realm.

She might even have been able to explain osmosis to a twelve-year-old. But would she ever have taken to a Fax?

THE DICKENS CONNECTION

It began with one of those early-morning exchanges, when the brain slips momentarily out of gear and the tongue carries on willy-nilly. The Middle Daughter had just emerged from her pit, unwashed and uncombed. Her black-spotted dungarees, worn with a green-and-purple rugby shirt, complete with ketchup splatters, were probably most charitably described as *arresting*. The Old Feller caught sight of her and re-named her Magwitch.

This wasn't quite appropriate, but I knew exactly what he was getting at. Everyone at the breakfast table liked her new nickname. They'd never heard it before. When the Old Feller asked them: 'And who was Magwitch?' no one could tell him. Well, I did put my hand up. I said, 'Sir, sir! Me sir!' But he told me to hush up and eat my toast.

The Heir Apparent thought Magwitch was a Polish football team, and the Junior Daughter wanted to know 'BBC or ITV?' The information that Magwitch has no connection with Indiana Jones or the Top Twenty hit them very hard indeed. How could they possibly be expected to identify him? Then I told them that he was a character in a book and that I was pretty sure the story had once been dramatised for television. Their spirits rose. Having ascertained that we were not talking Shakespeare, they beamed straight in on Dickens – a simplistic view of Eng. Lit., but on this occasion a useful one.

Attaching herself like a limpet to the only bit of Dickens she knows, the Middle Daughter wouldn't be budged. 'He's the clanking one that frightens Scrooge. It's Christmas Eve and I think they take a turkey round to Tiny Tom's. What's that got to do with my dungarees?'

The Senior Daughter wasn't so sure. She thought she smelled a *bicentenniel* connection. Could it be that fly cove who lurked outside Tellson's Bank between grave-robbing assignments? Or the lady designer of radical hand-knits with the season ticket for public executions?

They got it eventually and I was relieved that the guessing was over. I had *Great Expectations* and *David Copperfield* hopelessly and horribly mixed. One question about Miss Havisham and I'd have been done for.

The librarian I overheard the next day was not so timid. '*Tarka the Otter*? Try under T.' 'Will that tell me who wrote it?' 'Nobody wrote it. It's the book of the film.'

At least she didn't think it was a Polish football team. Give the girl her due.

CAPITAL GAINS

Thanks to the generosity of a gadabout Gran, my children have been globe-trotting since they were just out of nappies. But the Senior Daughter and the Heir Apparent have just experienced an entirely novel adventure. They have made their first unaccompanied trip to London.

Parents whose children brave the North Circular every day of their lives will wonder why I consider this worth reporting. I must ask them to imagine how forbidding Finchley can look when you're standing on the edge of the Fens.

When they asked for permission to go the only reasons I could find for refusing were that London is big, dangerous and full of wicked cynical people who are up to no good and I didn't raise my children on mother's milk and country air to expose them to risk so casually. Even Gran, who has taken Calcutta, Bombay, and Margate on a Bank Holiday Monday cheerfully in her stride, thought it all a bit risky.

But in six months' time the Senior Daughter will be old enough to elope to Gretna Green. If she wants to elope by tractor, she will be old enough to drive it herself. I got a grip on myself and agreed to the proposed trip. In return they promised to stick together in adversity.

They caught the 9.15 slow train. At 10.30 they called to tell me they had *arrived*. 'I don't want to know you've *arrived*,' I whimpered. 'I just want to know you've come home safely.' Their money ran out before I could remind them about muggers, steamers, sewer rats, slave-traders, and the price of a small cup of coffee. All morning I wondered whether they'd coped on the Piccadilly Line, or stayed on, paralysed with fear, all the way to Heathrow. I went to the library and tried to work.

When I got home they were there ahead of me, feet up, kettle boiling. 'Welcome back,' I said, 'and so soon!' 'Well,' said the Lad, 'it was like this. We'd seen everything, and it makes your feet ache, so we thought we'd make tracks.' Actually, they hadn't seen *everything*. They'd seen Covent Garden.

They'd taken a long, admiring look at all those strutting hairdressers and seriously stylish youths in black leggings. They'd bought some wonderful cheap shirts and a pair of nasty earrings. And they had got the hang of automatic ticket barriers.

No rats had been sighted. No press-gangs, and no thuggees. But they had seen the price of a small cup of coffee. And knowing when they were well off, they had remembered the way home.

October 1989

CLASSIC MISTAKES

The Department of Education's report on the status of Classics in Britain's schools, just published, tells of a subject devalued, barely holding its ground, reduced in many cases to being taught After Hours. A sad tale? Perhaps. But certainly a complex and interesting one.

In the two secondary schools attended by my children, Classical Studies and Latin are available and popular, Greek not so. In neither school is Latin open to all comers. It is an option given to those who have shown considerable aptitude in the learning of French. The message is clear. Latin is difficult.

But Latin isn't difficult. My own experience of learning it was that it was no harder than French. Personally, I found Mathematics and Physics to be far more intellectually searching. Later in life Logic defeated me so roundly that I'm convinced one of my cerebral wires must have worked loose, and in the matter of languages, the Cyrillic alphabet still makes me falter. While I'm ponderously spelling out P-R-A-V-D-A, Michael Buerk has told two more news stories and said Goodnight.

A lot is claimed for Classical languages. Chiefly that they encourage clear thinking and accurate use of English. My memories of two years spent monotonously declining by rote are that with practice a state of Nirvana is reached. The mind floats pleasantly, contemplating Jam Roly Poly, and the voice carries on regardless. I would have thought that if schools are in favour of Clear Thinking, then they should teach Clear Thinking, or at least make a better job of teaching Mathematics, which would achieve the same thing.

And an improved grasp of English, of how it was created? It's rare for me to finish checking any piece of journalism without opening my dictionary and being reminded that our language bubbled up from a ferment of many others and my own work often owes more to Atlantic Avenue, Brooklyn, than it does to Horace.

To understand where we've come from is important. But we also have to understand what we are now and what we may become, and since Time and the Core Curriculum wait for no one, can someone tell me what's wrong with using good translations? Wouldn't it be much wiser for all children to read Thucydides *and* Graham Greene and never to open any book without first switching on their hogwash detector?

I haven't a tear to shed for Classics. If they're done for, it's the classicists who dunnit. You could call it unfortunate. But tragedy would be a better word.

CAT CALLS

I'm not in good odour this week. I got rid of the
lodger and everyone else wanted him to stay. I'd
made it clear from the start that it was only till he
found a more suitable billet, but no one thought I
really meant it, and if I'd said, 'It's him or me, take
your pick,' it's safe to say I would now be trudging
down the street with a sleeping bag strapped to my
back.

The first thing was that a tiny black kitten woke
us with his cries. He was trapped in a neighbour's
courtyard, and although there were overhanging
branches and all sorts of feasible escape routes,
somehow he just couldn't work it out. The Heir
Apparent climbed a ladder and lowered a rescue
bucket, and as the bucket cleared the wall the kitten
inside it had a look about him that said: 'Great! A
kind lady *and* a heroic winchman, all in one family.
When's breakfast?'

At that point I knew two things about cats. I knew
that I liked them. And I knew that keeping one was
out of the question in our present situation. We live
in a city centre. Double-decker buses shudder past
our front door day and night. We have no garden,
no tangled shrubs for hiding in, no trees for getting
stuck in. Some people do keep cats ten floors up in
Manhattan, but to me that has always sounded like
a raw deal for cats and assured income for cat psy-
chiatrists.

I only went out and bought flea powder, worm
pills and cat food to tide him over until someone
read the notice in our window and came, overjoyed,

to claim him. For his part, he sat each afternoon alongside that notice, mouthing to interested pas- sers-by. 'Lost? Who's lost?' So far as my children were concerned he had his paws well and truly under the table.

I refused to give him a name. I gave him a ping- pong ball and that was as friendly as I was prepared to be. The Junior Daughter drew him, the Middle Daughter photographed him, and the whole family conspired against my efforts to keep him safe and get him adopted fast.

The day he moved out was a dark day indeed. I told him he was going to half an acre of mature gardens, generously stocked with shrews and mice, but he didn't look very thrilled. And I learned some- thing new. Even when you don't give a cat a name, once he's allowed you to have him on your lap, saying Goodbye is a tough assignment.

The trouble with me, as one small cat will testify, is that I have a kind face and a heart of carbor- undum. But I'm certain it was for the best. I've only kept a can of food just in case. Just in case of what, I'm not so sure.

FIGHTING CHANCE

Two American mothers, much-praised in their own land, are about to be published in this country. *How To Stop Your Children Fighting* is described as essen- tial reading for parents who would otherwise resign themselves to the inevitability of bickering children. A book for me, clearly.

The techniques promoted by Mrs Faber and Mrs Mazlish evolved from workshops at which parents and children discussed their family feuds. Workshops have come a long way, haven't they? When I was a child a workshop was a place that smelled of machine oil and Woodbines.

People who live in glasshouses are advised against throwing stones – though if they insist on doing it I suppose we could ask them why they did it and how it felt – and I should therefore cover myself by saying that there are many people who earn a pleasant living by doing something insignificant and I count myself in. I am nevertheless surprised that workshops on quarrelling children have found any takers, even in the United States.

How can anyone busily rearing children have the time or the energy to try dismantling complicated sibling relationships and putting them back together in an improved form? Aren't small people supposed to pick up clues about the world at large by sparring for a few years in the miniature world of family life? The more I read the more convinced I became that what we have here is yet another manifestation of the Urge To Meddle.

The authors recommend that parents use their more mature command of language to help a child express his negative feelings. 'Why didn't Annabel come fitted with a zip on her mouth?' could, with a little well-meant adult tweaking, become 'I think your sister needs to know how she irritates you. Why not draw her a picture of how you feel?'

I could see the appeal of this kind of tinkering; channelling hostility in the direction of creative safety valves – in a sense it's what I was doing when I gave the Middle Daughter an extra pillow to punch – if I didn't have a stronger faith in the value of non-interference. The world is full of irritating people. Several billion at the last count. And childhood, especially shared with brothers and sisters, is the perfect crash course in human relations.

Better to learn something with Annabel's foot in your ear, I'd say, than seated in a workshop. Don't these people have any floors that need scrubbing?

HAPPY RETURNS

Parenthood is punctuated by hurdles. The road ahead may look clear and then just around a sharp bend you're asked to clear Frustration and Disappointment in quick succession. People I know who've lived long enough to watch their children draw the Old Age Pension confirm what I've suspected from the start – that the trickiest hurdle of all is the one labelled Letting Go.

With this in mind I have tried hard never to think of myself as indispensable. Daily, without fail, I forget. I run from room to room, gathering up dirty socks, making dental appointments, comforting the downhearted, and dealing sternly with the disobedient. I try to do the work of half a dozen people and only occasionally and apologetically ask the Old Feller to do the work of two.

On the eve of my departure for foreign parts I let it slip my mind yet again that I am not sole custodian of the lore of wash cycles and frozen dinners. I ironed and cooked. I made lists of emergency phone numbers. And I took time out to worry that someone might lose their dinner money or break a leg. No self-respecting child, it seemed to me, would arrange to get into major difficulties when I was around, if they could wait and do it *after* my 737 had taken off.

In fact, in my absence a great number of unusual things occurred. The Middle Daughter rose each morning with a smile on her lips and a song in her heart. The Heir Apparent worked out where clean shirts come from. Nothing got lost, bungled or broken, and, as if all that were not enough, Gran arrived with an apple-corer and a tin of custard powder and set about preparing Some Proper Meals.

I did not come home to chaos and recrimination. I came home to fresh flowers, furniture that smelled of polish, and children with clean, shining hair. There was no fetid tangle of towels on the bathroom floor, and I had dried my hands on my skirt before I noticed that the towel rail was in use. The writing on the wall could not have been clearer. They had done very nicely without me.

Five days after my return the process of backsliding was complete. Shoelaces were snapping, light-bulbs were popping, and highly important school forms were going AWOL from my desk.

I asked a friend, 'Why do I have to leave the country before my children will eat cabbage and hang up towels? Why do I feel put-upon when I'm here and superfluous when I'm not?' 'Ah!' she said, 'That's called Being A Mother.'

December 1989

FESTIVE SHADES OF BLACK

I've always thought Christmas trees look best heavily laden with just two or three colours. We've had many red, green and silver Christmases, and last year we were silver, pink and purple, but I'm no martinet. When the Junior Daughter came home with an end-of-term offering in orange and blue, I didn't spurn it. I never saw a colour scheme yet that wasn't improved by the maverick touch.

The whole glittering phenomenon, which goes up absolutely no sooner than December 20th, is always topped by a cardboard angel. It was made for me by the Heir Apparent when he was a very little boy indeed and it was an apposite gift. The concept of angels interests me. Ours looks more like he just came in from the night shift than from the edge of the ether, and his hair, once abundant and woolly, is now reduced to three grey strands.

I have refused all offers of new angels, and I will not have a fairy. I don't care if it's a tradition. It's not *my* tradition and I will not accommodate plastic upstarts on top of my tree. Besides, I like an annual reminder that my son was once a cherubic innocent. Now he's gaunt and towering. He taps along to the kind of music you can't tap to. And he paints things black. First his bedroom ceiling. Then his fingernails.

I called up a friend who knows about these things. She's had two punks and an anorexic and they turned out all right in the end. I said, 'Gran will be arriving any day now and the only begotten grandson is wearing black nail varnish.' She asked if he'd dyed his hair black as well and when I told her he hadn't she said, 'Sounds like a very mild Gothic interlude to me. Make sure he gets plenty of Vitamin D and don't force him to do anything jolly. It'll be over before you can say Gormenghast.'

I put it to him. I said, 'Are you wearing black nail varnish to provoke me, or are you making an important statement about yourself?' 'Yes,' he said, 'I'm a Goth.' So I thought I'd better discover how Christmas goes down amongst the pale and gloomy. For a start, I don't think he'll want the clockwork dentures that walk along a desk top, or a tightly rolled copy of *Whizzer and Chips*. The whole point about being a Goth is to look intimidating. It doesn't do to chortle or titter.

I'm not counting on him for fireside carols, and I don't expect him to wake me at dawn because he thinks the red parcel might be a dumper truck. But on the quiet, I'm hoping the brandy butter may make him forget himself.

I said, 'Are you an Ostrogoth or a Visigoth?' 'Dunno,' he said, 'which sort wears black eyeliner?' *Pax vobiscum.*

January 1990

THE CINDERELLA SHIFT

Life is a party. Don't quote me on this. I'm only repeating what I overheard. The Senior Daughter and the Heir Apparent, having made a bulk purchase of spray-on hair glitter, are now fully paid-up members of the Pleasure Party. I'm the one who stays home with the pumpkin.

Of course, this is a seasonal flush. By February they'll be mooning around on a Saturday night waiting for *The Les Dawson Show*. The torrent of invitations will have calmed. There will be no need to draw straws for the only dry pair of jeans. And I shan't need to ask such irritating and impertinent questions as 'Where are you going and who are you going with?'

This kind of interrogation is an affront to teenage dignity, but who cares about that? The streets are full of broken glass and ruthless people, and clearly I need to know that my children are not compromising their own safety in the interests of appearing cool, I also need to know that they're not out there mugging old ladies. Those awkward questions have to be asked, even if the answers are impenetrable.

'Whose party are you going to?' 'You know Mauler, who used to go out with Lorraine before she started going out with Tosh . . . well Mauler's sister knows these people and it's their second cousin's party at Upper Wapshott Village Hall and everyone's invited.'

'So you're going to Upper Wapshott?' 'No. We're all going to Tania's to get ready, then we're walking round to Gazzer's, picking up some amplifiers, and then meeting Scottie, Grunter and Badger's Breath at the bus station. *Then* we're going to Upper Wapshott.'

When I've examined Grunter and Gazzer's pedigrees, and ascertained that the village hall has not been licensed for jelly, ice-cream and cocaine derivatives like some of these aircraft-hangar finger buffets one reads about, we have to crack the hardest nut of all. 'Since you have to be home by eleven and neither your father nor I are looking for a career in mini-cabbing, how are you going to travel?'

The answer is nearly always spelt TAXI. I don't really have that kind of money. They certainly don't have that kind of money. And taxis are not infallible. Quite often they come late. Sometimes they don't come at all. All it takes is a bit of bother on the B1297, or the chance of a fat little earner someplace else, and there you are, stuck in Wapshott without wheels.

I sit up for them. I read Miriam Stoppard's Problem Page and the small ads, and wait for the sound of a key in the door. And every time it happens I conclude that there's only one solution. I must stop being modern. I must discreetly and soberly chaperone them everywhere they go. Life is not a party.

ERROL'S FLING

The Junior Daughter had a hamster for Christmas. But only after she had served a long apprenticeship of Wanting a Hamster. She, and we, have now moved on to Phase Two. This is called Living With a Hamster.

There's something I should tell you. I may as well get it off my chest now, as have it hanging over me for the next five paragraphs. His name is Errol. It isn't really worth explaining why. Persuaded by the fact that hamsters don't need baths, five-mile hikes, or live maggots for dinner, I sent the Old Feller shopping for a cage and someone to live in it. He returned with the ultimate des. res. – a confection of plastic and metal designed by someone who has unravelled the hamster psyche and is no slouch at marketing either. This rodent palace, this South Fork amongst hammy houses has the lot. Tunnels to explore, snug sleeping quarters to remind the modern hamster that his forebears slept in holes beneath the Syrian desert, and an exercise wheel, for keeping us humans awake at night.

On Christmas Eve, while I made much ado about dinner being served, Father Graham smuggled him in. The Senior Daughter was sworn to secrecy. 'You're sharing your room with a top-secret guest tonight. Blab and you're grounded.' So on Christmas Day Errol was a complete surprise. A completely surprised surprise.

We got on famously. He slept those long, contented sleeps I used to imagine human babies slept, and when he surfaced he did everything with relish.

The Junior Daughter twittered to him through the bars. Soon, we promised her, he would know her well enough to submit to a cuddle.

It's hard to be patient when you're ten. Sometimes you just can't stop yourself taking off the lid and trying to hurry love. One fine morning Errol had gone. 'Stop that hamster!' I shouted. 'Shut all doors, block all drainpipes!' Every Jeremiah in East Anglia dropped by to tell me I was wasting my time. Errol, they assured me, would be halfway to Harwich. But I knew. Somewhere, in a heap of old dust-sheets, or a pile of old lambswool jumpers, he would be holed up, awaiting a dignified rescue.

It was mid-morning when we nobbled him, sizing up a baseball boot as a temporary billet. 'What did you think of the world then?' I asked him when he was back inside Fawlty Lids. 'Big, isn't it?' he whispered. And then, as an afterthought, 'Shouldn't you be sobbing with relief?'

A WORLD TO THE WISE

We've been busy with the atlas, what with the Senior Daughter being five months off GCSE Geography and not knowing where to find Chile. Apparently they don't do *that* kind of Geography these days, but I wasn't fobbed off so easily. I don't see the value of writing brilliant essays on urban planning if you wouldn't know Santiago from a sack of anthracite.

'Bring me your school atlas,' I told her. But here's

another thing. She doesn't have a school atlas. She has never known the pleasure of flicking idly through and stumbling across the River Po. The girl hasn't lived.

I reached down the family atlas and the Senior Daughter sighed. She's seen me get lit up about this kind of thing before. It eats into the evening and before you know where you are you've missed *Coronation Street*. The Junior Daughter joined us. As things turned out I'm glad she did. If you're hoping to learn something it's always as well to have a percipient little truth-seeker sitting on your lap. 'Cor!' she said, 'Greenland's big!'

Here was I, in the nineteen-nineties, showing my children the world according to Gerhardus Mercator.

I've nothing personal against Mercator. I'm sure he was a very clever man and I expect his mother was proud of him. But he's been gone nearly four hundred years. Cartographers can now make better maps than he did and if I'd only thought of it I could have invested in one of them. It would have saved me peeling a tangerine in a homespun effort to prove that Greenland is not bigger than Africa.

'We're lucky,' said the Junior Daughter 'We're right in the middle of the world. If this big pink country was in the middle, we'd be on the edge. And we're quite near the top. If you live in Australia, does it feel like you're near the bottom?' I wasn't qualified to say.

Ethnocentricity is a challenging subject for a small person, leave alone for a small mother who's had a long, hard day with the vacuum cleaner. 'I'll buy a globe,' I said. 'Then you'll be able to see that there isn't really a middle or an edge.' And to give the Senior Daughter a break in her rambling search for Chile, I showed them both a few places they'd have heard of. Memphis, Tennessee. Torremolinos. And Bethlehem.

The Senior Daughter had one question for me. 'Can I leave Chile till tomorrow?' The Junior Daughter had two. 'Which page is Heaven on? And can I eat the tangerine?'

I love an enquiring mind.

WORDS FOR EATING

The Middle Daughter has been doing one of those projects where you have to write down every single thing you eat and then your Biology teacher gets the Social Services sent round to see whether your mother ever heard of a balanced diet. *Or*, your mother makes you doctor the evidence with the insertion of a few fictitious salads.

The truth of the matter is that a perfectly good nutritional mix is available in our house. For fifteen years I've been offering my children lightly steamed broccoli that has been tossed in butter and shown the nutmeg. Year in, year out, I have the broccoli dish to myself. Also the cabbage, the cauliflower, the peppers, green and red, and of course the spinach. I dine nightly with five people whose idea of a vegetable is ketchup.

I had hoped that when puberty began to ravage

their complexions and true love stirred, they would see the error of their ways. I thought they'd say, 'Just the ratatouille and a glass of spring water for me!' instead of increasing the Clearasil budget. But it hasn't happened. They look in magnifying mirrors and howl. And still their favourite meal is a large pile of garlic bread followed by a large pile of chocolate ice-cream.

Saturday Breakfast, wrote the Middle Daughter, *pain au chocolat. Saturday Lunch, kich*. 'What's the meaning of this?' I asked her. 'I didn't give you quiche for lunch.' 'No,' she said, 'I made it up because I wasn't sure how to spell macaroni.' *Saturday Tea, Egg and Chips*. It's always egg and chips on Saturday because that's when the Old Feller cooks and egg and chips is what he does best. Sunday is when I stuff mushrooms and everyone looks shifty.

Sunday Breakfast, she wrote, *Bacon, waffles and baked beans*. How I wished I'd got up earlier to slice a fresh pineapple. Or poach a bit of smoked haddock. Too late. No hole in the ground opened up to swallow me and my shame. I vowed to try harder. Sunday Dinner, I decided, would be the saving of the family's reputation. A little vegetable soup, a robust goulash, a bit of greenery that had flirted briefly with oil and vinegar, and to follow, fruit *ad libitum*.

I cannot tell by what sleight of hand the greasy roast potatoes appeared. My mind is blank over the deep-frozen chocolate cake. One minute I was chopping parsley, while my family menaced me with threats of eating out. The next, I was doing something shoddy with an Oxo cube.

Some day I may commit a crime of passion. I may run off with someone who eats lettuce.

FAME AND MISFORTUNE

Clive James lives round our way. We're not actually neighbours. If I needed to borrow a cup of sugar or jump-start the car he would not be the first person I'd look to, but we do see him knocking about from time to time and in a city famed for its heavyweight intellect he does help to give the place an air of frothy celebrity. After all, he's on the telly.

The Heir Apparent is phlegmatic about this kind of second-hand glamour. He once had his cricket bat signed by Viv Richards and frankly life's been a bit of an anticlimax ever since. And the Senior Daughter is practically a legend in her own school playground. First Year boys with scrawny necks and gaping shirt collars dare each other to speak to her. They shout, 'Oi! My friend likes you,' and 'You're that girl that sings in a band. My brother says you're rubbish.' She seems to attract the younger fan.

Anyway, the Old Feller and the Junior Daughter were out for a stroll, when Clive hove into view. The word was passed from pedestrian to pedestrian, 'It's Clive. He lives here. Act natural. Act *completely* natural,' and everyone was behaving in a strenuously abnormal way. They were all looking into the gutter.

'We saw a little fat man,' said the Junior Daughter. 'He's called Clive James and we didn't stare at him.' Now what is the point of carrying on like that? What is the point of Clive finding the courage to face the television cameras if viewers aren't going to rush up to him outside the paper shop and say, 'Saw the show. I don't care for Australians myself but the wife insisted. Actually, people always say *I'd* be a natural on the box.'

If Clive had wanted a quiet, anonymous life, he'd have stuck to writing books. We writers shuffle around all day in our slippers. We run to the pillar-box without brushing our hair and argue with shop assistants, free of the burden of being recognised. Our readers wouldn't know us if they saw us. This all comes as a great relief on mornings when you can find nothing to wear but your gardening trousers.

When I get letters from readers who want to be writers and who ask my advice, I always tell them: 'Do it. Buy an exercise book, sharpen your pencil and be a writer.' Now my attention has been drawn to Clive, who can't nip out for a bottle of milk without people vigorously ignoring him, I'd like to add, 'And whatever you do, stay off the telly.'

February 1990

FAG ENDS

It was midnight. The house was quiet and decent folk were fast asleep. The perfect time for acts of treachery and cowardice.

If *you* were in thrall to a despicable addiction, if *you'd* promised your loved ones that you'd got the habit beaten, but you were fibbing, wouldn't midnight be the hour you might be found, lurking behind closed doors, careless of everything save the relief of abandoned indulgence? In short, a crafty fag in the kitchen.

We were eating with friends. They were both in their second week of kicking cigarettes and they were doing it because the children had asked them to. Their children, like mine, belong to a generation that's had every chance to see smoking for precisely what it is. These children are fearful for their parents' health. Our children feel the same way about their father's lungs, but our Old Feller's solution has been to take his habit and all its accoutrements, and confine them to his office. The only thing he brings home is the smell.

Perhaps if we hadn't talked about smoking the evening would have turned out differently. We chatted about Norman Fowler's resignation, logical positivism, and the best way to cook leeks. But at every turn there was a pull towards the forbidden subject. Plainly, we were dining with two people who were desperate for a smoke.

I blame the Old Feller. He need never have told them he had the weed about his person. And if they'd discovered it by frisking him casually as he passed the potatoes, he could still have been a true and constant friend. He could have said 'Don't give way now. Think of the children,' and to display his solidarity he could have ground that pack of cigarettes beneath his heel.

Nothing would stop them. As I reached for a second helping of my own chosen chocolate-flavoured poison, the three of them lit up. They inhaled, they sighed, they spoke in tongues, and frankly they hallucinated beyond the bounds of decorum. They also forgot about the smoke alarm. No family should be without one. Theirs is thirteen years old, male, and equipped with nostrils that never sleep.

'How could you!' he said. 'Hand them over!' Caught in the act, his parents were bashful but defiant. I filled my mouth with chocolate pud and distanced myself from their middle-aged delinquency. There was a tussle. He won because he's strong and healthy and doesn't have a smoker's cough. He took their filter-tip comforters away from them. 'Some day you'll thank me for this,' he said.

I wonder where he learned a line like that?

LIFE LINES

The Junior Daughter is doing a Sponsored Recite. She has a poem to learn, her nearest and dearest are being asked to promise money for each line correctly remembered, and the school library gets to benefit to the tune of several much-needed pounds. Of course we agreed to take part, just as we did with the sponsored walks, the sponsored silences and the sponsored fasts, because our children enjoy the feeling that through their own actions and decisions they are materially making a difference. My own feelings about it are far from joyful.

There are two things bugging me. One is that my daughter has only been asked to learn a poem by heart because the school is short of brass. By the time I was eleven years old I had a repertoire of poems I could be called on to recite. Learning by heart was a regular feature of my classroom days.

We learned Keats and Wordsworth. In our music lessons we learned 'Nymphs and Shepherds'. In assembly we learned 'Cinquering kongs their titles take'. And at home the process carried on. I learned 'The Pied Piper of Hamelin' from my father and with a bit of prompting can remember it still.

My children have never wanted to listen. At school they don't sing hymns and they never wonder 'Who is Sylvia?' In thirty years' time they won't put their brains through the hoop of recalling their old school song because they don't have one. Only the Junior Daughter may fumble around for the next line of 'Excuses' by Allan Ahlberg, because way back in 1990 she was promised 20 pence for each line she memorised. That's my other quibble – that I have my hand in my pocket yet again.

I have always expected to pay for the jam on my bread. For outings, parties and all other jollies I've taken it as read that parents who can contribute should do so as generously as they can. Having chosen to educate my children exclusively in state schools I do not ask for the moon. Only that they have the raw materials of learning: teachers, paper, pencils, instruments, scientific and musical, and books. At what point on the road to cost-effectiveness did a decent school library become a dispensable luxury?

'Excuses' is a lovely poem. Now the Junior Daughter has cleared the hurdle of learning it, she has relaxed and seen the very funny side of it. I'm still on tenterhooks. I'm awaiting the sponsored Hop to Land's End to pay for a teacher's salary.

SENT PACKING

The Lad and I are just back from Venice. At fourteen I thought he was ready for the excesses of Carnevale.

'We're travelling light,' I told him. By which I meant we are only taking that trusty canvas cabin bag that sufficed for me round the world and back again. In this way you can cock a snook at people who send you to Italy and your suitcase to Venezuela.

I advised him to take walking shoes, and in due

course he presented me with a pair of gnarled and malodorous sneakers. I wrapped them in polythene, put them in the bag and guess what? The bag was then full. My cunning plan had already run aground on account of the size of the boy's feet. I provided him with a cabin bag of his own. 'Pack it,' I said, 'with everything you require for four days of normal, run-of-the-mill *dolce vita*. We'll organise the masks, the jewelled turbans, the brocades and the black silk domino when we get there.'

So off we went. A travel-size middle-aged woman and a gangling youth with a copy of *Melody Maker* under his arm. La Serenissima didn't know what was about to hit her.

'Where's the toothpaste?' he asked me before bed the first night. 'Well,' I said, '*my* toothpaste is here, in my bag. I wouldn't know about yours.' I allowed him to use mine of course. I'm not a vindictive woman. Nor an especially fastidious one, but I did have to stop him in his tracks as he dressed for Mass in St Mark's. 'Not that T-shirt!' I bellowed, 'You slept in that!' 'I know,' he protested 'but it's clean.' It was clear I had to go back to basics.

'First,' I said 'Slept In is Slept In. Take it off. Second, the elderly parishioners of San Marco are not ready for Heavy Metal psychedelia, so any T-shirt worn will be covered by a *proper* shirt buttoned to the neck. And third, the whole hideous assemblage must be encased in a nice warm woolly because in the Basilica, spiritual uplift is integral with hypothermia.'

We had an action-packed visit. Some of it was the kind of action you see in the bottom of a slowly-drained coffee cup, but we did get out there and do our stuff. Mosaics? We seen 'em. Canals? We smelled 'em. And posers, rakes and dandies? We clocked them all as they paraded past us, and they clocked us, the Heir Apparent dressed as Something Black and Rumpled, and me dressed as Somebody's Mother.

'Where's the shampoo?' he asked on our second night.

Next week, Dicing With Death in Venice, Part 2.

DEATH IN VENICE

As travelling companions the Lad and I should be most compatible. We both like watching people, eating regularly, and staying up late. We both have low saturation thresholds for religious monuments, and we both rather like boats, as long as they're not the flimsy kind that will only stay upright if someone hangs over the side in an exhilarating manner. With all this in mind I drew up our Venetian itinerary.

My trade-offs were designed to keep us adequately stoked up with culture and food. A mooch round a basilica full of stolen property – a sort of *Sack of Byzantium* edition of *Crimewatch* – 'Could this twelfth-century incense burner have belonged to someone *you* know?' – earned us dinner. An hour's homage to Tintoretto and Titian was worth another hour seated in a suntrap with a jug of hot chocolate. Not quite how Ruskin would have done it, but there we are.

Sometimes, in spite of Venice being in top form, the Heir Apparent looked tired and glum. He was missing his sisters. He was missing his usual Saturday pilgrimage to Andy's Records. 'Buck up,' I said 'Have an ice-cream. And while you eat it I'll amaze you with some interesting and gruesome facts.'

So while he revived himself I told him the tale of Admiral Bragadino, who came a cropper with the Turks and got sent home from Famagusta in a very small parcel. First they cut off his nose and ears, then they dangled him from a yardarm, and after ten days of public degradation they skinned him alive beneath the midday sun. And there's more. Eventually his hide found its way back to Venice. Cleaned, blessed and neatly folded, there it now rests, in a little urn in San Zanipolo.

Visibly perkier, the Heir Apparent followed me onto a Number 20 vaporetto. There was something across the lagoon I thought he might enjoy.

I was right. On the isle of San Lazzaro, an urbane and charming Armenian monk who breaks his vow of silence Thursdays and Sundays, 3 till 5, led us to an upper room and the inspiring presence of a mummified Egyptian princeling. He still has some of his teeth. More than three thousand years old and he's got more gnashers than the Old Feller! My son was most impressed. While I moved on to admire a monastery library that contains Voltaire, and a computerised polyglot printing press, he lingered by that embalmed body and thought his own thoughts.

He says it was better than the Grand Canal. I guessed he would. Somehow we mummies just know.

March 1990

NOISES OFF

I would like my next two teenage children to come fitted with volume control knobs. I've already had a word with the Middle Daughter about it but she doesn't think such an operation can be done. As far as she knows, erupting into loud bumptiousness is an integral part of becoming thirteen. Can this be true?

The Senior Daughter was a late developer. She was fully fifteen and a quarter before she invaded the furthest corners of the house with Dogs d'Amour playing at full tilt. And she might be a nice girl yet, retiring early with her stamp collection and a mug of cocoa, had it not been for her baby brother. Overnight he has become too big for his father's boots, and too noisy for anyone equipped with normal hearing. The Senior Daughter thought it looked like fun.

I don't expect to like their music. My own parents thought The Kinks were a waste of space. If Doris Day was good enough for them they figured she was certainly good enough for me, and even when my taste evolved towards Bach my father thought it rum to go in for tunes you couldn't quickstep to. So I am used to that kind of cultural isolation. I'm happy they've found some music that makes them happy. I just don't want to hear it, especially when I'm behind a closed oak door and wearing earplugs.

It isn't only the music. The telephone never stops

ringing, and it's never for me. They have long conversations in the nineties equivalent of Goon Show
voices, with people they only saw an hour ago. They
ask each other things like 'What are you doing?' and
the reply is always 'Nothing much really,' but it takes
a long while to say. And then, when their ears start
to get hot and achey from the telephone earpiece,
they invite everyone round so that any unfinished
business can be dealt with face to face.

My house is full of other people's teenagers. They
burst through my front door in braying waves carrying guitars and cassette tapes, toothbrushes, sleeping
bags, birth certificates, National Insurance cards,
and long-stay permits. That's when the noise level
seriously takes off. 'Hi!' screams the Senior
Daughter, 'Who cut your hair? Can you stay till
Easter? I've got so much to tell you!'

I predict they'll all be deaf by the time they're
forty. Then, sadly, they won't be able to hear Bach.
But they won't be able to hear their teenagers either.

ON BEING A SUNBEAM

Copious thanks this week to the guardian angel of
Journalists Stuck For a Story, who presented me
with Bernard, the director of a course of musical and
dramatic improvisation for ten-year-olds. Amongst
them, the Junior Daughter and her chums.

For three days they lived in a lovely old country
house. They roamed its gardens, queued for the tuck
shop and tittered in the dorm. But chiefly they spent

their time creating A Musical Happening. An invention for voices, instruments and bodies in sweaty little leotards, directed – no – *enabled* by Bernard. I think Bernard would like to be remembered as an enabler.

We were invited to attend an evening performance. Sixty parents who had hurried home from work and not had time to eat, assembled themselves on sixty of those bum-numbing chairs unique to school halls and listened while Bernard said a few words.

I must paraphrase. Bernard is really into the concept of the totally developed brain. So am I. He

thinks left-handed people have a better balance of activity between their two cerebral hemispheres. So do I, and so do a lot of neuro-physiologists who know more about it than I do. I'm just not sure that Ringo Starr was the most inspiring example for Bernard to choose. Still, he did also mention Mozart, who was brilliant at billiards and wrote a few good tunes as well.

What Bernard was getting round to was that we shouldn't expect too much, that the Musical Happening would have rough edges, and that as an audience we should work *with* it and not *against* it. One or two men shifted in their seats and wondered whether they'd be home in time for *Brush Strokes*.

In the first bit the Junior Daughter extemporised on a xylophone while some human snowflakes thundered past. Bernard told us when it was time to clap. Then followed a much more elaborate creation. Lumpen girls with orange streamers pretended to be sunbeams, the Junior Daughter did thirty self-conscious seconds as a waterfall, and a chubby chap in paisley pyjamas tried to be a mouse. It was not good theatre.

I don't mind men with maracas earning a living this way. And I'm happy to pay for my daughter to join in, because she did enjoy it. But watching it was a painful intrusion into the private world of Bernard and his sunbeams. In fact if he'd asked me, I could have done him a lovely squirming gooseberry. Improvised, of course.

CHEAP THRILLS

From where I'm looking this has to be one of the most cynical weeks of the shopping calendar. Small fry everywhere are emptying out their piggy banks, only to find that the writers of florists' price-tags have thought of a number, then doubled it.

I watched the Junior Daughter balancing the books. On £1.20 a week, she's barely recovered from Christmas and she has a sister's birthday up and coming. But first there's Mothers' Day. Even if I increase the going rate for polishing door brasses and pegging out washing, even if she robs Peter to pay Paul, the Chocolate Kabin, and W. H. Smith's Greetings Cards Department, she's still not going to manage. And I hate watching her try.

When I was a girl Mothers' Day was called Mothering Sunday. If you went to church you brought home a tiny bunch of violets and presented them to Mother as she sweated over a hot Yorkshire Pudding. The chances were it was business as usual in the kitchen, but if she'd had tea brought to her in bed that morning, slopped and sloshed from cup to saucer as the stairs were mounted, she considered herself the most cherished of women.

I came in for plenty of cheap cherishing myself when my own children were young. Someone decorated a twig with paper blossom. Someone else drew me a dinosaur on roller skates. And I always got extra rations of kisses from little people who really needed to have their noses wiped. It was lovely. And it didn't cost them a bean.

Now we have big business. Belgian chocolates,

silk roses and potted palms. Cards that drip with unctuous verse for 80 pence a throw. Do you want them? I don't.

Here is my blueprint for a glorious Mothers' Day. I'd like the Senior Daughter to put the top back on the pickle jar and not drip her tea bag all the way from the mug to the dustbin. I'd love the Heir Apparent to take his coat to the dry cleaners and clip his toenails. If the Middle Daughter would get rid of the ten plastic carrier bags that lie under her desk, and eat one meal without slurping I would be truly thrilled. And if the Junior Daughter and Errol the Hamster can jointly manage to spring clean without a trail of sawdust and sunflower seeds from here to eternity, my cup will probably runneth over.

Of course, if anyone's in the mood for giving, I'd kill for another skating dinosaur. And a replacement blossom twig would be simply champion.

CAMBRIDGE BLUES

The 136th Boat Race is about to be contested on the Thames and for the life of her the Middle Daughter cannot understand why. It seems perfectly reasonable to her that it should happen in Cambridge, or at worst in Oxford. She has difficulty understanding leap years as well. And the putting forward of clocks.

The River Cam is our backyard. Lacking a proper garden, it's the place we go to when we're feeling cooped up, or at odds with the world, and the Middle Daughter, more often at odds than at peace, spends a lot of time on the riverbank arguing with herself. She watches the college eights as they train. The rhythm of the blades soothes her. And it hasn't escaped her notice that she is the perfect height for a cox. At the moment.

There is every indication that by the time she's of age she will have eaten her way to stroke position.

'Coxes don't have a lot of fun,' I told her. 'While the big boys are pigging-out on suet pudding and Guinness, little Miss Cox is nibbling raw carrots.'

She broke off from finishing someone else's pasta to remind me that her previous career plans had foundered for exactly the same reason. Flat-race jockeys aren't allowed seconds of spaghetti either. She could see at least one reason why. 'I suppose I might make the boat sink,' she said, and then, rather taken with the idea, 'Has anyone ever sunk? Do you want that piece of bread?'

I told her how I'd seen Cambridge slip beneath the water in 1978. She was nine months old then, bouncing on my knee with a rusk in each hand. I just missed 1912, when both crews sank.

She has now decided to transfer her support from the home side to Oxford because she prefers the colour of their jerseys, and to start thinking in terms of career opportunities for the short but solid.

I predict she will become a bollard of society.

April 1990

WINDS OF WAR

The Senior Daughter came home two hours before curfew on Friday night. I wish I could say I was pleased.

We've spent the last two years congratulating ourselves for moving to a city just as our children outgrew duckponds and tricycle trails. They'd had their fresh air, and the countryside was filling up with a hooligan element in pink jeeps. We packed our bags and came to live in a city whose country roots were still discernible; the people smiled and said 'How do!' and you could walk the streets at night in safety.

As the Senior Daughter and the Heir Apparent matured we gradually allowed them more rope. So long as we knew where they were going and who they were going with, so long as they stuck together in adversity, we gave them a cheery wave and thanked our lucky stars we weren't living in the Bronx.

Friday night was different. With her brother away, the Senior Daughter went out alone, to meet friends. Someone suggested a stroll. So they all pulled on their black greatcoats and flapped off down the street like a rookery out on the razzle.

They strolled into the arms of the enemy, another wandering band of shiftless youth. They call themselves Ravers, and their identifying marks are that they wear bright-patterned clothes and waggle baseball bats at people in black. The chief identifying mark of the people in black was that they were scared. A fight broke out. The Senior Daughter ran home in tears.

There is nothing new under the sun. Me and the Old Feller are of the Mods and Rockers generation, though neither of us was ever involved. I was too busy with 'O' Levels and he just wasn't allowed. We dealt with the crisis calmly. Made her wash her face, then got the motor out and went for a tootle round the streets to make sure none of her friends was lying in a gutter.

She seemed to absolutely see our point – that to people who are not quite right in the head, a group of teenagers identically dressed is a kind of provocation. She agreed that the unfairness of the situation was irrelevant, and that when there's trouble on the streets, you stay home.

By morning she'd changed her tune. Handing the city over to airheads was a cop-out, she'd decided. And if she wanted to look like a moulting crow, no one was going to stop her.

I thought it was probably the Weetabix talking. But we grounded her anyway, just in case.

YESTERDAY'S CHILDREN

As I prepare to wear a different journalistic hat, I've been looking back through the 'Generation Games' scrapbook.

Three years ago, when I dished up that first helping of family dirt, I was actually dwelling in a green and pleasant land. The Senior Daughter was thirteen, the baby of the family was only eight. They were, I reported, quite a handful. They grizzled at bedtime, lost their plimsolls, and categorically would not eat cabbage.

And yet they weren't so bad. They still lived in a world where teacher was God and Mother was God Almighty. They still had their mittens attached to dangly strings. Caring for them was not so much a challenge, more a piece of cake.

Now they have grown. The Senior Daughter is old enough to marry. She's not going to. She's leaving school, going to college. Her evenings are spent singing Fats Waller and wearing larkey costumes. Mine are spent worrying about crack, and alcohol, and the kind of men she's definitely not ready for.

Her two sisters have been caught in the wash of her metamorphosis. Inevitably they demand more than she did and at an earlier age. They don't necessarily get it. With her we were feeling our way. Our grasp of things is firmer now. We have met the enemy and she is a teenager who cannot see the point of anyone older than twenty-three.

Daughters are a worry, it is true. But for now the Heir Apparent represents the most spectacular frustration of our hopes. His maturation has been meteoric. Six months ago he was a boy. He owned a whoopee cushion. And he rated girls a poor fourth in importance after the English test squad, the publishers of *Wisden's Almanack* and the manufacturers of Gunn & Moore bats.

Today he is a very big boy indeed. He dresses in a notably challenging style, and relishes nothing so much as a run-in with minor authority. If we didn't live in England I suppose this is about the time someone would take him to a jungle clearing and teach him how to catch his dinner. What urban ritual will mark his passage into manhood? Ten pints of lager, a chicken vindaloo, and an ill wind that blows no one any good?

I must thank them anyway, for three years of 'Generation Games', nobly borne. They are the four most interesting experiences of my life so far and, like a pack of cards being shuffled before my eyes, they change all the time. In truth, they never cease to amaze me.